Henry's All Blacks

Henry's All Blacks

MURRAY DEAKER

with John Deaker

HarperSports
An imprint of HarperCollins*Publishers*

National Library of New Zealand Cataloguing-in-Publication Data
Deaker, Murray.
Henry's All Blacks / Murray Deaker with John Deaker.
ISBN 978-1-86950-668-1
1. Henry, Graham. 2. All Blacks (Rugby team) 3. World Cup
(Rugby football)—(2007—France) 4. Rugby football coaches—
New Zealand. 5. Rugby Union football—New Zealand. l. Deaker,
John. ll. Title.
796.333092—dc 22

Harper*Sports*
An imprint of HarperCollins*Publishers*

First published 2007
HarperCollins*Publishers (New Zealand) Limited*
P.O. Box 1, Auckland

ISBN 978 1 86950 668 1

Cover design by HarperCollins Design Studio
Photographs by Jo Caird
Typeset by Springfield West
Printed by Griffin Press, Australia

79gsm Bulky Paperback used by HarperCollins*Publishers* is a natural,
recyclable product made from wood grown in a combination of sustainable
plantation and regrowth forests. It also contains up to a 20% portion of recycled
fibre. The manufacturing processes conform to the environmental regulations
in Tasmania, the place of manufacture.

Acknowledgements

Our thanks to the hardworking team at HarperCollins — Lorain Day, Eva Chan and Sandra Noakes; our gratitude to the eagle-eye of editor Teresa McIntyre and our special thanks to Jo Caird for her superb photos, which have added immeasurably to this book.

Contents

Foreword

There were no special favours from the All Black camp. Henry said, 'The All Blacks have a certain mysticism about them which is one of their strengths that I want to make sure stays in place.'

NEW ZEALANDERS AREN'T MAD about rugby — they are totally obsessed by it. Rugby is not only their national game, it is their 'reason for being'. It is a game that suits their personality — uncompromising, pragmatic, physical, structured yet innovative and intuitive.

The changes in society based on their social welfare state, along with ever-increasing political correctness, have turned New Zealand from a country based on a proud, independent, pioneering spirit into one where too many of its citizens are looking for a hand-out; where all are subject to excessive government regulations and interference in their lives; and where instead of a quest for excellence there is now satisfaction with mediocrity. In all things except rugby.

Rugby is stronger now than ever before. It is a tangible link to the past, when men in black from a minute colony in the Antipodes would journey north to the Home Country and teach the English how to play the game they had invented. Any self-respecting Kiwi will be able to recite the folklore of the 1905 Originals and the 1924 Invincibles.

It is quite simply the greatest rugby nation in the world. For a period of time, South Africa rivalled and even bettered it, but apartheid and neutral referees changed that.

Against this background, the quest to win rugby's World Cup has assumed the proportions of a national crusade. The inaugural event of 1987 was staged in New Zealand and won by the All Blacks, but since then the William Webb Ellis trophy has been held by countries to whom the game means comparatively little.

The campaign of 1991 was destined for disaster from the moment John Hart was paired up as co-coach with Alex Wyllie. Both men were outstandingly successful coaches of their respective provincial teams, but inevitably the tour party split into factions. The team had beaten itself before the Wallabies completed the process in the semi-final at Dublin.

In 1995 Laurie Mains' All Blacks were clearly the best team at the World Cup. The management, which included the personification of All Black rugby in Colin 'Pinetree' Meads and Sir Brian Lochore, made a major mistake in not getting the final postponed for a few days to allow the team to recover from what was widely believed to be a case of deliberate food poisoning. Add to that the impact of Nelson Mandela wearing a Springbok jersey onto the field for the final and, quite simply, the All Blacks were never going to win.

The 1999 campaign highlighted how desperate Kiwis were to win the World Cup, and how that desperation led to delusions. In 1998 the All Blacks lost five tests in a row and were hammered in Sydney by Australia just before the Cup. Yet when the team was humiliated by the French at Twickenham, the nation turned on coach John Hart in a fit of blood-letting that verged on mass hysteria.

By 2003 the All Blacks were back at the top of world rugby, and their form going into the World Cup suggested an England–All Black final. However, they succumbed to an average Australian outfit without really firing a shot. Coach John Mitchell was sacked and Graham William Henry became All Black coach.

It is against this background that this book is written. Originally I considered calling on my close relationship with Graham Henry to get the 'inside oil', but in a meeting with him in January 2007 he told me 'there will be no special treatment, no insider links. The All Blacks have a certain mysticism about them which is one of their strengths that I want to make sure stays in place.' It was obvious there would be no favours from the coach.

This was reiterated later by the All Black media liaison officer, Scott Compton, who basically told me I would have to take my chances alongside all the other journalists at media days. At least there was nothing new in that — I'd been doing that since 1996 and the advent of professionalism. Prior to that it was much easier to interview All Blacks and develop relationships with them. I had the home phone numbers of players like Sean Fitzpatrick, Zinzan Brooke, Grant Fox and John Kirwan, who were available for spontaneous interviews without the orchestration of a media liaison man.

This has proven to be a blessing in disguise. If I had been given 'insider' knowledge, I would have been compromised. Quite clearly, on reading this book you will realize it is written from an objective 'outsider' viewpoint. Not that I have been able to discount a forty-year relationship with Graham Henry, during which we have played rugby and cricket against each other, taught at the same school and socialized together. I believe I know much more about him than he knows about me — it is the job of a New Zealand broadcaster to watch the All Black coach more closely than a stockbroker studies the fluctuations of the market. However, we did enjoy a level of cooperation in describing the roles of the management team. This segment of the book is a direct response to the dozens of talkback callers who ask, 'What do they all *do*?'

Naturally the method of writing the book became different, although the objective remained the same. Instead of relying on information directly from the All Black camp, our conclusions were gleaned from rugby reports, rugby writers' views, the opinion of past All Blacks, and statistics.

I say 'our', because with access to the All Blacks limited it became obvious to me that I'd have to rely on a researcher. Fortunately I was already employing my son John in that capacity with my radio and television shows. It has been an interesting experience for one who has spent his entire life largely working solo to co-write this book, but one that has been pleasant and rewarding.

Much of this book was composed prior to the 2007 World Cup. It was always in the back of my mind that we might not win the World Cup — but win or lose, I believe there is a story to be told.

Murray Deaker

The Obsession

Obsessions only end when their cause is eliminated.

- When did the obsession start?
- Why do the All Blacks choke every four years?
- Will preparing differently break the habit?

FOR MANY NEW ZEALANDERS, winning the Rugby World Cup has become an obsession. Like most obsessions, it is unhealthy. This obsession manifests itself as the dominant topic of conversation for a wide cross-section of the population. Everyone — from plumbers, lawyers, teachers and accountants to carpenters, receptionists, dentists, wharfies and, of course, taxi drivers — has a view on how it can be won, and no two views are the same. All are world authorities on this subject, prepared to debate the topic for hour after countless hour. To most of them 'debate' means argue, talk incessantly, never concede, always be right, and most of all never listen to anyone else.

Kiwis are convinced they know more about rugby union than anyone else and they are equally certain their beloved All Blacks are the best team on the planet. The first assertion can never be proved or, for that matter, *dis*proved, so with typical Kiwi confidence it has become accepted as fact.

Which leaves the second assertion — that the All Blacks are the best team on the planet. Sadly for the Kiwis this can now be tested, and is — every four years. New Zealanders have only got themselves to blame for this, because they were the ones who pushed for, organized and hosted the first Rugby World Cup in 1987, in Auckland.

They won it then but at the next four World Cups they failed — and failed dismally on three of those four occasions. Even the most arrogant, ignorant, passionate and prejudiced All Black supporter began to see that it was illogical to assert the All Blacks were still the best.

Best what? Best chokers? Before 1991 no rugby follower would ever have thought of using the words 'choker' and 'All Black' in the same sentence. Along with the Springboks, the All Blacks had clearly been a dominant force in world rugby. With South Africa excluded from international rugby in the 1980s because of its apartheid policies, the mythical world crown was New Zealand's.

Myths are probably even more unhealthy than obsessions, and this particular one was shattered in the semi-final at Dublin in 1991, when a divided, ageing, unhappy All Black team was blown away by the Wallabies. Given the average New Zealander's severe inferiority complex about Australia, the result couldn't have been worse. After all, there was no getting away from the fact that Aussie Rules, rugby league and soccer all had more players than rugby union in Australia, and outside of New South Wales and Queensland, few people across the ditch even knew there was such a thing as a Rugby World Cup.

Culprits had to be found and blame allocated. It would have been far too easy to have just said Australia was better on the day and David Campese was the best player on the field. Heavens, no! No one is better than the All Blacks — they just somehow end up with more points! It wasn't hard for all of the country south of the Bombay Hills and north of the Harbour Bridge to find its culprit — John Hart and the Auckland faction. Most Aucklanders didn't really care, but the few who did reckoned Alex Wyllie was 'over the hill and had lost the plot'.

> **Before 1991 no rugby follower would ever have thought of using the words 'choker' and 'All Black' in the same sentence.**

The general feeling was that the Aussies had won by a fluke and it wouldn't happen again. A few people in the know questioned the way the team was selected, coached and managed, but they were viewed as theorists who didn't know what they were talking about. After all, this was the All Blacks and we were the best in the world. The best could be beaten by a fluke but certainly not by a better team or a team better prepared, coached or managed. Perish the thought that they might have better players.

This arrogance, which had permeated through the All Blacks, and indeed the entire rugby scene, was bred from an outstandingly successful record dating right back to the 1905 Originals. Their success, combined with that of the legendary 1924 Invincibles, established New Zealand as a great rugby nation. Kiwis who still referred to England as the 'Home Country' and weren't prepared to accept full independence from Mother England until 1949 were, however, willing and anxious to see 'their boys' dish it out to the Poms on the rugby field.

Because of this, rugby and the All Blacks in particular were pioneers in establishing some independence, some shreds of nationalism and the association of the colour black with New Zealand. All of this combined to raise the status of the All Blacks beyond that of a mere sporting team. In the eyes of many New Zealanders they were the greatest and could do no wrong.

Even their defeat by the South Africans in the 1995 World Cup final at Ellis Park did not shatter this delusion. It was explained away by the apologists, who blamed waitress Suzie for — allegedly — poisoning the All Blacks and Nelson Mandela for inspiring the Boks. There was little doubt that the All Blacks played some sublime football during the tournament, and Jonah Lomu was a sensation. At the end of the contest All Black supporters sought some solace in being beaten by a team with the only other group of supporters as fanatical as themselves — and at least it wasn't the Aussies!

However, fans were freely expressing doubts about the status of the All Blacks in world rugby, and this proved to be the penultimate step in the development of a full-blown obsession.

That obsession was finally born in 1999 with the defeat of the All Blacks by the French at Twickenham. This time there was no excuse. New Zealand rugby was humiliated, and an appalling lack of effort by the All Blacks in the meaningless contest for third and fourth only made matters worse. It quickly became known that the All Blacks had been under strict instructions from coach John Hart not to retaliate to any provocation from the French, who grabbed the open licence to kick anything and everything, push players off the ball and pinch their testicles. Those of us at the ground were surprised to learn that all of these misdemeanours had taken place, because our attention had been totally occupied by an All Black team that played without passion and brains and were deservedly beaten by an inspired side.

The New Zealand public hit on the lack of All Black retaliation for the perceived dirty play by the French. Talkback callers saw it as a slight on the national character — a reflection of the liberal approach in New Zealand schools; a result of women taking over the country; a predictable effect of giving the All Black coaching job to an Aucklander, especially one with a corporate background; an insult to those who had worn the All Black jersey in the past; and, worse still (if the callers were to be believed), an insult to those who'd never worn it but 'would give my eye-teeth and left ball to do so'. An illogical obsession of national proportions had been established.

No New Zealand killer, rapist, serial murderer, corrupt politician, bent businessman or child molester has ever been subjected to the volume and degree of abuse that John Hart copped.

In John Hart, coach of the All Blacks in the failed campaigns of 1991 and 1999, those most obsessed found their target. Certainly Hart had set himself up by occupying centre-stage in the lead-up to the 1999 Cup. He focused attention on himself, and it was clear before the event that if the All Blacks won he would be the biggest winner. People in the know spoke openly about both a knighthood and CEO of the All Blacks (Inc). Equally as obvious was that if the All Blacks lost, he was going to be the biggest loser. And he was.

No New Zealand killer, rapist, serial murderer, corrupt politician, bent businessman or child molester has ever been subjected to the volume and degree of abuse that John Hart copped. It reached its most absurd low when a horse Hart part-owned was spat at by some twits at the New Zealand Trotting Cup meeting in Canterbury. The vitriol continued for months on talkback radio, no matter what hosts did to try to change the subject.

Slowly Hart's name disappeared from the public forum, but the obsession about the World Cup continued to grow. By the time the next World Cup came round in 2003, most New Zealanders were saying the All Blacks would win it easily and that would teach 'them' a lesson. 'Them' was a collective term for the Australian administrators some ill-informed Kiwis illogically believed had cheated them out of a sub-hosting of the Rugby World Cup; the IRB who had changed the rules to combat All Black prowess at ruck and maul; and the Poms who were ridiculed for playing a boring, winning, ten-man style of rugby, just as the All Blacks had done for much of the 1950s and 1960s.

Once again the nation wasn't prepared for a semi-final disaster, particularly against an Australian team it had beaten 50 – 21 a few months earlier. Worse still, it wasn't going to accept another gutless, inept display by a team it knew could play much better. The sight of Aussie George Gregan casually advising Byron Kelleher 'four more years' was one no All Black fan will ever forget.

For the first time New Zealanders knew they weren't the best. They were shattered, traumatized, defeated and dispirited. All their lives they had been told they were the best . . . and the lie had been exposed.

Add to that the clear knowledge that the rest of the world *also* knew they weren't the best, and the fans were hurting more than ever. Worse still, a new name was starting to be tagged to the All

Blacks — chokers. Now this *really* hurt. The average Kiwi doesn't mind being categorized as a bit of a hayseed, may even acknowledge that he's not as worldly as a Pom or a Frog, but accuse him of gutlessness and you're in big trouble. However, your trouble would be minor compared with that of the average Kiwi rugby fan, who had no real defence to the accusation.

It was against this background of failed campaigns, despair and obsession that the NZRU appointed Graham Henry.

It was true that the All Blacks were the best team in the world *between* World Cups, but come the big one, on the world stage, the only result that counts — and the All Blacks choked. Suddenly, old-fashioned New Zealanders who all their lives had defended the concepts of win or lose; winning isn't everything, it's the only thing; and 50 per cent pass and 50 per cent fail in School Certificate started to point (without real conviction) to the mythical world rugby rankings where the All Blacks were always number one. Meanwhile, writers like Peter FitzSimons, with humour, and Welshman Stephen Jones, with cynicism, began to turn the screw marked 'Choker'.

It was against this background of failed campaigns, despair and obsession that the NZRU appointed Graham Henry. The Welsh had already anointed him 'Great Redeemer' and 'Henry the Great'. He would have to be better than *both* those titles if he was to win the Holy Grail with the All Blacks.

Redeemer . . . no. *Great* . . . not good enough.

This was a job for a Messiah.

The Messiah

There is little balance to Graham Henry's life. His ambition is only matched by his diligence. His goals are simple — to be the best coach he can possibly be and to coach the best team in the world. His mantra is 'Good coaches win'.

- Is Henry an over-achiever?

- How did he become so street-sharp?

- Why did he fail with the Lions?

IF SUCCESS IS JUDGED on how close one comes to achieving one's potential, Graham Henry must rate as one of our most successful Kiwis. Other people may have more flair, more intuition and more ability — but few, if any, have the tenaciousness, the street-cunning and raw ambition that have marked Henry's rise. His close friend, Chris Doig, describes Henry as 'the greatest over-achiever I have met'. This annoys Graham, who fails to recognize it as the ultimate compliment.

Graham Henry's success is built around his diligence, his extreme focus and his ability to pick the right people to support him. The hours he spends viewing tapes of not only his own team, but also those of the opposition, are legendary. His game strategies leave nothing to doubt.

One celebrated occasion was the planning he put into Auckland's 1996 challenge for the Ranfurly Shield against Canterbury. Graham assessed that one of Canterbury's real strengths was also its most vulnerable weakness — Andrew Mehrtens. Merts was vital to Canterbury's record, not only as a goalkicker but also as an attacker. Henry rightly assessed that if Merts could be effectively taken out of the game early by the application of specific pressure, Auckland was home. That day Andrew had a shocker. Every time he got the ball he got the Auckland loosies at the same time. Henry also directed Auckland to kick the ball over the dead ball line so that Canterbury were forced to re-start, time after time. It was dreadful stuff to watch, and probably led to the law change that quickly followed. But it was also basic, simple and highly effective, with the final score of 36 – 0 reflecting the strategy of the coach and its application by the team.

The hours Henry spends viewing tapes of not only his own team, but also those of the opposition, are legendary.

In a country where high-profile coaching positions far too often go to former All Blacks, many of whom had successful playing careers solely because of their intuitive skills and are bereft of objectivity and understanding of the game, Henry stands out like a beacon for the future.

This is a man who did his apprenticeship for the role of professional coach by putting in 30 years of amateur service. Graham's own rugby career was as a slow, ponderous, yet thoughtful first five-eighth, initially with the Christchurch Boys' High School first fifteen and later with the senior High School Old Boys team in Christchurch, the Union Club team in Dunedin and University in Auckland. What he lacked in natural athleticism he compensated for with rugby nous. He was much more successful in cricket, representing Canterbury as a wicketkeeper at first-class level and Otago as a batsman. To the outsider it appeared as though any coaching career would be in cricket, not rugby.

At Otago University Henry completed a Diploma of Physical Education, but more importantly he met Raewyn Cochrane. She was from a rugby family with two brothers, Bruce and Kelvin, who played for the Christchurch club for many years, with Kelvin representing Canterbury on a number of occasions as a loose forward. But not even two rugby-playing brothers could prepare Raewyn for Graham's fanaticism for the game.

Raewyn Henry is the perfect partner for a rugby coach. Her balance matches his intensity and her sense of humour brings him back to earth, but most of all her total support of her husband, coupled with their steadfast unity, makes them a formidable pair. Even more to the point, she understands sport and its demands. Raewyn has coached top netballers in the Auckland area and had a stint in charge of the Welsh national team. At Otago University she studied physical education and played a variety of sports. Raewyn is Graham's rock —

the glue that cements the family relationship. In choosing his most important partner Henry showed his great ability to pick the best person for the job, the same ability that would later be a feature of his coaching career.

Few wives would put up with Graham's intensity, his single-minded focus and his complete dedication to the task. Balance is not a personality trait of the All Black coach, but it *is* a predominant characteristic of his wife. Simply put, in rugby speak, without Raewyn, Graham would lose his play-maker, his goalkicker, his defence and his attack. This was a rugby marriage made in rugby heaven.

Graham Henry's rugby coaching career started with the Auckland Grammar first fifteen. Again, Henry chose wisely. Grammar has supplied over fifty All Blacks and produced some magnificent teams. However, when he took over as coach Grammar was struggling and hadn't won the competition for many years. Henry enjoyed immediate success and quickly developed a squad of players whose skill and style made them the most talked-about team in town.

Up until this time no one in New Zealand was coaching the flat backline that had been so successfully pioneered by Australia, with Mark Ella to the fore. Auckland Grammar had two sensational speedsters on the wing in Mark Henley-Smith and Peter Beguely. They were so quick that they finished first and second respectively in the New Zealand men's open 100 metres. Under Henry's tuition, Grammar flicked the ball along the line to give the two speedsters space on the outside. It was revolutionary, and so different that ill-informed critics were heard to remark, 'Imagine how much better Grammar would be with a deeper backline.' Even at this early stage Henry had learnt the advantage of selective hearing — he didn't listen.

Two first five-eighths of outstanding ability were the focus of the early Grammar sides. Both were to become All Blacks. Nicky Allen was like a central character out of *Boy's Own*. Hugely talented in all sports, Allen's skills with hand and foot coupled with his quicksilver running made him an exceptional player. With Henry's tactical strategy, Allen became quite simply the best five-eighth seen in secondary school football in decades.

And then along came Foxy — much more a Henry-type five-eighth, being also blessed with a brilliant rugby brain. Even at sixteen Fox was like a chess master in the way he moved Grammar around the field and expertly pinpointed the opponent's weaknesses. The Henry/Fox relationship was a meeting of like minds, of similar personality types and kindred spirits. It is difficult to determine who benefited more — suffice to say it was a partnership that set both careers on an upward spiral.

Under Henry's tuition, Grammar flicked the ball along the line to give the two speedsters space on the outside. It was revolutionary.

Graham was appointed to the physical education department at Auckland Grammar by a man who had taught him at Christchurch Boys' High School. Former All Black captain John Graham had just been given the job of headmaster of the great school.

John Graham, better known as D.J., was already a formidable character before he arrived back in Auckland, but his appointment to Grammar, the country's most acclaimed high school, led to him becoming the most significant and controversial figure in education in the late 1970s and the 1980s.

D.J. Graham has had an extraordinary influence over hundreds of young New Zealanders, but few owe as much to him as Graham Henry. It was D.J. who had persuaded Henry to use his talents at university by studying physical education — originally Henry had thought he would study history. John Graham is a canny evaluator of men, and considered Henry to be unsuitable for straight academic study unless it was closely linked to athleticism; hence phys-ed. It was not to be the only time D.J. Graham was to shape the life of Graham Henry.

Henry has always enjoyed making money and in this, like his rugby, he is prepared to gamble. He left his first position on the staff of Christchurch Boys' High School for Golden Products, a pyramid selling scheme that quickly became horribly unstuck. In the early 1970s you didn't leave a secure profession like teaching for a pyramid selling scheme without some of a less-than-golden product sticking to your reputation, but D.J. Graham stepped in and offered Henry a lifeline. Along with Raewyn and the kids, Henry left the closeness of two extended families in Canterbury and headed for the City of Sails.

It would be difficult to overestimate the impact D.J. Graham had on G.W. Henry. Suffice it to say there were times when Henry appeared to be a younger clone of the great headmaster. Even today, when Henry is confronted by testy reporters he sticks his jaw out — and for all appearances he's a carbon copy of his old boss at Auckland Grammar.

For the young Henry, D.J. Graham was mentor, confidant, close friend, adviser and evaluator. Graham gathered around him a group of young staff nicknamed the Magnificent Seven, who gathered every Friday in the boss's office to discuss a range of subjects, principally rugby. This group included Dave Syms, a very good Auckland hooker at the time; Steve Watt, the Auckland prop whose goalkicking prowess earned him the title 'the Otahuhu Adding Machine'; and Chris Doig — opera singer, Auckland hockey representative and later CEO of New Zealand Cricket, who knew nothing about rugby but was the most eloquent of them all.

John Graham probably knows Graham Henry better than anyone and is ideally positioned to comment on him, and in the preparation of this book I quizzed him at length about Henry, the man. What follows is a record of those conversations.

John, what are the strengths you see in Graham Henry as a coach?

Graham has a deep knowledge of the game in all its dimensions, developed over many years. He's coached a wide range of teams and done the hard yards — school, club, colts, representative and finally the All Blacks. He's experienced all the emotions involved in coaching rugby teams. He spends countless hours researching his own team's strengths and weaknesses and the individual needs of his own players to assist the team and the individual to perfect their games. He does the same analysis of the opposition, and this process gives him a detailed knowledge of what he wants his team to do. He has a fierce, dedicated tenacity to win. 'Coaches have to win,' he says constantly.

Graham has a total focus on the task ahead, and as he builds up to the game ahead he becomes more and more introverted and intense. He comes to each game constantly worrying about whether he's done enough to prepare his team. He has the ability to choose very able management and coaches who complement each other and he uses them accordingly, insisting that each one does their job.

Is he a good selector?

He has become a very good selector. I think in his younger days he had favourites and occasionally couldn't see past them. Through his Welsh experience especially, he's developed the ability to spot a player and how that player will fit into his team. He uses video technology superbly to confirm his thinking or impressions of a player he is interested in. He has developed these selecting skills to a very high degree.

What are his weaknesses?

He over-complicates the game. He is introverted as a person and he could express the joys of life more to his players. I think his tenseness used to get to the team and affect its performance. That's gone.

He has got to learn to give more of himself. He has a talent to use people and perhaps should touch base with those that help him. I can understand that weakness because he is so focused. He has a lot of good friends, and a small number of important close friends.

Is he a good critic of his own coaching, and does he know his own strengths and weaknesses?

He understands when things haven't gone well but I don't think he is aware of how other people see him, particularly how his team sees him. He has, however, worked hard at that and is much better than he used to be. He has had to adjust quite markedly to endear himself to his players. They respect him and admire immensely his dedication and work ethic. Many aspire to the same work ethic — that is a real strength he has. Great coaches are not loved by their players, but *are* respected and trusted. In the end that is more important. Perhaps as time passes those players he has coached so successfully will have more than respect for him.

Is he the best coach of a rugby team that you've ever seen?

He is as good as you'll get. He's been fortunate to coach talented sides from Auckland Grammar right through to the All Blacks. For example, he took over Auckland at the height of its powers, with brilliant personnel like the Brooke brothers, Fox, Fitzpatrick and Jones. Therefore the trip to Wales was quite pivotal in his coaching development. In Wales he found there wasn't the talent he was used to and he had to coach more individual skills, more tactics and more strategy. It was there he became a great coach. I think he also learnt the 'don'ts' of coaching when he took on the Lions — it bruised him. When he returned from Wales he was the complete coach.

Is he equipped to handle defeat at the Rugby World Cup, and the consequences?
The expectation we are going to win puts huge pressure on him and the team. Everything points to the fact that they're equipped to handle that. However, most years the All Blacks drop a crucial test and they have continued that under Henry in 2005 and 2006. That would be shattering.

How would a person so focused and introverted deal with such a public failure?
He understandably would find that very difficult. This is his moment. He's had so many great coaching experiences, and he has become a fabulous coach. However, this is the defining year for Graham Henry. As far as I am aware everything he has asked for from the NZRU has been granted. There are no outs! It would be shattering personally for him and his team if they do not win the World Cup, but I believe he now has enough experience to cope.

The Friday night chat sessions at Grammar were full of robust debate and Henry thrived on them, testing theories that the following day his first fifteen would put into practice. Most rugby-playing New Zealand males believe they played in 'the best first fifteen the country has ever seen', but those who saw Graham Henry's champion sides at Auckland Grammar are quick to acknowledge that in fact they were second-best. Huge crowds gathered at the Mountain Road ground to watch the action as word spread that something special was happening.

Alan Faull, a former journeyman lock with Teachers rugby club in Auckland, was the first fifteen manager at the time, working alongside Henry. 'Without doubt he is the best schoolboy coach I've seen. He was totally analytical. What was different from all the others, though, was that everything was focused on winning. The secret to his success was that he had good people around him — at the same time, he was good for those who worked for him.' Faull remembers being sent by Henry to a St Paul's practice where he secretly filmed all their moves.

Even at this stage Henry was showing his adaptability, taking a development team to Fiji where the opposition played without boots. There were five future All Blacks in the team, including the Whetton twins, John Buchan and John Mills. The coach was only interested in whether a skinny fourth-former could do the job without boots. 'Can you kick goals without boots, Foxy?'

Grant could and did, and Grammar won — in fact they won forty-two interschool games in a row.

Success leads to expectations of a good result, and success in rugby became a habit for Graham Henry right from the very beginning of his coaching career. Coaches are judged solely by their win–loss ratio, and Henry's stacked up. From the start he had good players, some of them brilliant. As always his timing was perfect — the greatest rugby school in the country had been struggling for the best part of a decade, despite the raw talent it had available. Quickly and expertly he turned them around with a minimum of fuss.

The young coach was quickly noticed by one of the wisest heads in Auckland rugby. R.H. (Bob) Graham is the brother of D.J. Graham. Bob captained Auckland during its famous Ranfurly Shield era of the 1960s, and many critics consider he should have been an All Black. He had played club rugby for University and recognized in Henry the coaching ingredients he considered appropriate to bring some structure into the notoriously disorganized University senior side.

With Henry on board as coach, University went on to win

championships with a team full of former Grammar pupils — and Grammar Old Boys was no longer a force in Auckland rugby. Here too Henry showed his keen selector's eye for spotting talent coupled with his own high level of work ethic. The University forwards, led by a young Sean Fitzpatrick, set about demolishing packs that had traditionally treated 'the students' as cream puffs.

At the University club Henry again renewed his liaison with Grant Fox. Fox wasn't every fan's favourite; North Harbour fans, in particular, were hard on him, pushing instead the attributes of Frano Botica. The difference was substantial, though — Fox was a match-winner with an accurate goal-kicking boot that quickly took University to Gallagher Shield success in the Auckland championship.

The University forwards, led by a young Sean Fitzpatrick, set about demolishing packs that had traditionally treated 'the students' as cream puffs.

Fox has very clear ideas about Henry's abilities, which came out in the following conversation:

What are the most notable ways that Henry has developed as a coach?
His people skills have developed markedly. He's always been a good analyst and an astute rugby brain, but when he was busy working as a headmaster during the day he was at times curt and abrasive. When he came back from Wales he had particularly developed new skills in handling people. You can't overestimate how much he developed as a result of the Welsh and Lions experiences. He treats people much better now.

Do you think he has peaked yet?
I don't believe he ever will because he is driven to be better — he's always searching for ways to be better.

31

Some people have said he's selfish. Do you think he is selfish or focused?

Definitely focused. I think selfish is too strong a word. In my book that's not a criticism. To get to the top you need to look after number one. Now he's got the top job and he wants the ultimate prize.

Do you think he's a good selector?

Very astute. He's always been prepared to promote young talent. Toeava didn't work initially but has shown good signs since. He brought Carlos [Spencer] to Auckland and made him. He takes calculated risks, yet I don't think he's a gambler. I think he can see the future — he can see where the game is heading and look at the talent needed to play it that way.

What do you think are his strengths?

His analytical ability — he is a great student of the game. Now he is also brilliant at managing his resources. He puts a good team around him and uses them well.

And what are his weaknesses?

It's hard to identify them now. He doesn't have the communication weakness and man-management weaknesses he used to have now he's got time.

What did Graham Henry do for your rugby?

I owe him heaps because he picked me for the first fifteen in my fourth-form year at the end of the season. I had three years with him in the first fifteen, and we won three championships. Then he convinced me to go to the University club with him — we played in two finals in '83 and '84, winning in 1984. I think it was a meeting of minds — he developed me and made me think about the game. I don't think I'm a clone of his, but I would never underestimate what I owe him.

Tell us about the early years at Auckland.

He had been incredibly successful with the Auckland Colts —
a large number of players became All Blacks. He took over
Auckland when they had been very successful. He showed
courage in changing that team — it wasn't easy to drop Terry
Wright, A.J. Whetton and Bernie McCahill.

I remember a meeting of senior players at D.J.'s place where
this new coaching staff pointed the finger at us and said we
needed to widen our approach. We challenged that. Don't
forget Trapp and Williams coached Auckland ninety times for
eighty-six wins, one draw and three losses. They had loosened
control . . . and it was successful. I thought Graham was wrong
and that the young guys were as bad as the senior players.
Anyway, we sorted it out.

**Do you regret not taking on the All Black coaching job with
him?**

No, I don't. I found coaching difficult — I struggled with the
nervous side. As a player I had an outlet; coaching gave me
no outlet. In 2003 Graham, Wayne Pivac and I were coaching
Auckland and I told him I was going to chuck in the coaching.
He said, 'I'm not surprised, former players struggle with the
emotional roller-coaster.'

When he applied for the All Blacks job he asked me to be his
backs coach. He said, 'Foxy, it's just a bigger roller-coaster and
it will be a hell of a ride.' He tried again later to get me to coach.
I think he made a great choice with Smithy — I think Smithy
is better in that group than me. I also think it is Smithy's right
position. He was never comfortable as a head coach.

Few Kiwis work as hard as Henry. He is driven by raw ambition,
totally ruthless in his quest to be the best. At times some of his

closest friends feel he 'uses' them. There are times when he wants information about a specialist topic, and he's not scared to ask. Graham has always had the ability to identify key people and ask the right questions. What's more, he is not afraid to go back again and again, seeking clarity.

There is more than a hint of fanaticism to the working Graham Henry. Icy intensity, ferocious focus and determined diligence mark his approach. In this he is not alone. Great coaches like Phil Jackson, Vince Lombardi, Fred Allen and Arthur Lydiard were all renowned for their single-mindedness, their determination, their steely focus and their ambition. Henry is no different. At times he can be unreasonable, curt, intolerant, humourless and even rude. These times are usually before a game when things aren't going well. Then again, show me a surgeon who's all smiles when faced with a tricky patient, or a barrister with time to chit-chat just before summing-up in a murder trial. Henry is no different from any other professional — a man prepared to do anything to get the best possible result.

Few Kiwis work as hard as Henry. He is driven by raw ambition, totally ruthless in his quest to be the best.

Being 'professional' isn't foremost about money — it's about attitude. Graham Henry was a professional rugby coach the first time he put his tracksuit on and walked out to take Auckland Grammar — the only element missing was that he wasn't paid. Professionalism for Henry means tireless endeavour, countless hours poring over videos, endless trudging from practice to practice, incessant seeking of advice, private sessions with players, countless phone calls . . . he never stops. He did this for twenty years without pay, and if really pushed would probably do it again under the same conditions.

Ambition is a much-maligned characteristic. Without ambition we have no chance of reaching our potential. Unquestionably all leaders — and that is what a coach is — need it to succeed. Graham Henry is to ambition what Muhammad Ali is to egotism, the Virgin Mary to purity, Al Capone to ruthlessness and Marilyn Monroe to sexiness. It is the essence of his being, his driving force, his raison d'être.

This was never more clearly illustrated than in his desire to coach Auckland. In 1990 he daringly challenged Maurice Trapp and All Black legend B.G. Williams for the Auckland coaching position. This would have been acceptable if they had been doing a poor job, but the previous season Auckland had won all of its nineteen games. Some of the players on the fringe weren't happy and Graham used that to mount a campaign that made some cutting criticisms. He later admitted he was ashamed of his actions, and certainly Maurice and Bryan, two fine rugby men, were hurt by it.

At the same time as the move to University, Henry had assumed the role of headmaster at Kelston Boys' High School, and within a short period of time the Westies knocked Grammar off its perch as Auckland's most successful sports school. This might not seem worth mentioning to those outside of Auckland, but try to imagine Tasman beating Canterbury in rugby and you'll begin to appreciate its significance.

More importantly, the shift to Kelston took Graham away from the white faces of the eastern suburbs to the brown boys of the west who, together with other Maori and Polynesians, would make up such an important component in future Henry teams. Henry remains in awe of their talent. 'Inga Tuigamala is the best secondary-school rugby player I've ever seen. Daylight is second,' he adds. Henry's love of the physicality of the Polynesians unquestionably grew from his experiences at Kelston, which many recent All Blacks — Mils Muliaina, Sione Lauaki and Mose Tuiali'i — also attended.

It seems amazing that anyone could coach Auckland and run a high school of over 1200 boys at the same time. In no small part this was achieved by Henry's great skill of picking good people to assist him. Steve Cole became his deputy at Kelston; he was later to succeed as headmaster, first at St Paul's Collegiate in Hamilton and then at St Bede's, in Sussex.

In appointing Rex Davy as manager of his Auckland team, Henry struck real gold. Davy is a salt-of-the-earth worker who calls it direct and straight. He can sniff out phoneys before they know he's on to them, and his loyalty to Henry was similar to that of Tonto to the Lone Ranger. In fact, Rex may very well be from the Wild West, the way he hobbles along.

It seems amazing that anyone could coach Auckland and run a high school of over 1200 boys at the same time.

I asked Rex to reveal some of what makes Henry tick:

What qualities did Henry have then?
His best quality was that he never had tickets on himself — he just wanted to coach at the top level. He had a passion for coaching. He was an attacking coach who loved to score tries.

Is he conservative?
He's a gambler. He wielded the axe in 1992 and brought in Craig Dowd and Robin Brooke. It was a calculated gamble to drop some great players and bring in new talent. I often used to say to his father, 'I can't believe he's your son because you're such a nice person.' His mum used to say, 'Why don't you smile on

television?' In Dunedin the camera flashed on Graham, and he waved at it and smiled as he mouthed, 'Hi, Mum.'

What was his greatest victory?

Undoubtedly it's the Canterbury Shield challenge of 1995 when Auckland won 35 – 0, and the fact he had worked out that by kicking the ball dead it nullified Merts.

What was his greatest victory with the Blues?

I think beating Natal in Durban in 1996 . . . we'd played Transvaal on the Tuesday and played poorly to be beaten. Natal became a must-win match. That was the first time we didn't jump in the lineout. Graham worked out we needed to push them back behind the line of advantage and use Michael Jones to bowl over Honibal and the two other loose forwards. On our lineout we threw the ball to Michael at the front of the lineout. The vital try by Eroni Clarke came as a direct result of pressure on their lineout. This game set the standard for the semis and the final.

Why is he so successful?

He's honest. He trusts people. For example, he always listened to D.J. Graham. Henry has never been a one-man band.

One of his greatest strengths is analysing the opposition. I don't know of anyone who works so hard. He watches videos right through the night. He had to do that when he was working as headmaster of Kelston.

He's prepared to change. On top of that he has vision and can see what is going to happen next in the game.

Did he change players' lives?

Yes, Carlos Spencer. He was out of the sticks, in his teens, a bit of a rough diamond. Graham created in Carlos' mind a map of the field — a way of playing. Junior Tonu'u was another. Both these players never played as well for any other coach.

What was he like before a game?
Very quiet. He went into himself.

Has he changed?
Yes. Because of his experience in Wales and with the Lions
he's different . . . he's far more polished. I could not believe
the development in him from 1998 to 2003 — that Lions tour
was difficult for him but it taught him a lot. He's always said
he shouldn't have coached both the Lions and Wales.

If he loses the World Cup, will he cope?
That would be difficult. He's put such an emphasis on it that
he's put himself in a corner. He's always coped in the past.
He's lucky . . . he has good people around, a wonderful wife
and some good mates, and I could never see the All Blacks
turning on him.

Auckland rugby quickly learned that Henry was prepared to make
changes when he sacked two very popular players, both former All
Blacks. A.J. Whetton and Bernie McCahill were almost institutions in
the blue-and-white jersey, but both were past their use-by dates. The
new coach didn't hesitate, and the other squad members realized
that no one's position was secure.

His first Auckland training was a real experience, one John
Graham remembers clearly. 'We met at Auckland Grammar School
and assembled in the normal way. Henry did the warm-up before we
broke into forwards and backs. I admit I was a bit nervous with some
great players there that I didn't really know. So we went through the
normal drills starting with lineouts. I said a few things first, and they
basically totally ignored me. They looked at me like I was a foreigner
from outer space.

'Then we went to scrums, and I talked a bit about scrummaging which I knew a little bit about. Once again I was totally ignored. They just went about their own stuff as if I wasn't there. After training I asked Graham how he'd got on with the backs. He said it was bloody difficult. They weren't really interested in what he had to say at all. I told him it had been worse for me — I was virtually ignored. Graham called a team meeting a few days later in which he proceeded to give an outstanding speech about what he intended his role coaching this team to be. He made it quite clear that those who didn't want to fall into line could leave. It really was a very impressive speech, and after that there were very few problems.'

In his time coaching Auckland from 1992 to 1997, Henry took them to victory in four consecutive Air New Zealand NPC titles, from 1993 to 1996. In '96 and '97 he also coached the Blues to Super 12 titles; the following year they were beaten in the final.

Henry's ability to assess the opposition was never more clearly highlighted than during a Japanese coaching experience D.J. remembers.

'Graham and I went to Japan and coached at Waseda University for a short time, where we looked after a group of highly intelligent young Japanese students. The first time we went along to watch them train, they ran around the paddock for half an hour with their captain for their warm-up. It was a disaster. We had an interpreter with us from Auckland Grammar School, so Graham pulled the team together and totally changed the way they trained. They were due to play against the University of Keio, who they hadn't beaten in years. Henry put in a request for some video of the Keio team. Once we'd both had a look, he told me we could stuff these guys.

'As it turned out we beat them easily, about 43 – 10. From there we stayed on for two or three weeks and won every game. That stint was a prime example of Graham Henry's coaching at its best. He totally changed their tactics and had tremendous success. What he did was look at the strengths of the playing squad — a very good halfback and first-five and a pretty useful pack — and organized the team's play around them. Once he'd made his changes they played some great rugby.

'We went back there briefly later on in the season. They ended up making the final, and if Graham had been there I'm convinced they would have won, after having come from pretty much nowhere. That was when I realized he had some very special talent as a coach.'

Henry's exit from the New Zealand coaching scene was done with panache. A hurried press conference was called at an Auckland hotel, and opened by Graham with the words 'I'm off to Wales . . . and I'm off tonight.'

Raewyn was with him, and the media revelled in an atmosphere free of NZRU and ARU blazers. Consequently the press he received was totally supportive, and it remains Graham Henry's finest hour with the media. Totally relaxed, he laughed and told them all they needed to know — except the figure Wales had paid him.

That stint was a prime example of Graham Henry's coaching at its best. He totally changed their tactics and had tremendous success.

Henry's announcement might have pleased the media but it certainly didn't please the powers-that-be at the NZRU or the ARU. It led to the NZRU introducing a rule which barred coaches who had taken positions overseas from coaching the All Blacks. At the time the press dubbed this the 'Henry clause', and it was widely rumoured that Henry had had to pay his way out of his contract with the ARU.

Not that everyone in Wales was keen to see an outsider as coach. A number of former players thought it was an insult that someone who hadn't even represented New Zealand as a player had received their country's plum rugby job. They failed to see that this was a coach close to his peak. He had won four NPC titles with Auckland and two Super 12 titles in a row — narrowly missing the hat-trick in a closely fought contest with the Crusaders at Eden Park. Basically, there was nothing left for him to do in New Zealand rugby — except coach the All Blacks. He was desperate to make the step up to international level and the path in New Zealand seemed to be blocked.

Welsh rugby at the time was in a dreadful mess. They had been defeated by France by 50 points, humiliated by England by 60 points and thrashed by South Africa by 96 points. Coming to this team was a huge risk, and most other coaches wouldn't have made the move.

A number of former Wales players thought it was an insult that someone who hadn't even represented New Zealand as a player had received their country's plum rugby job.

Acting quickly, Henry turned the Welsh team around. In his first game against the Springboks, at 28 – 20, Wales was unlucky to lose. He didn't have to wait long for his first victory, though. It came against Argentina — a team that had always been too strong up-front for the Welsh. This initial success didn't continue, with defeats following against Ireland and Scotland, but it was encouraging. The real breakthrough came with victory over France in a great display of running rugby in Paris.

The next opponent was England. There is no doubt that the Welsh measure themselves against England. What happened was beyond their wildest dreams. Neil Jenkins won the match with a conversion from wide out, and Henry was immediately hailed as the saviour of Welsh rugby. Titles like 'Messiah', 'The Great Redeemer' and 'Henry the Great' were showered on him, and adulation poured in from all quarters.

At a more realistic level, many of the Welsh players saw Henry as the person who had turned Welsh rugby around. In particular, he got the best out of players like Chris Wyatt, Craig Quinnell and Neil Jenkins.

Shortly after these early Welsh successes, the New Zealand cricket team toured the United Kingdom and Henry's old friend Chris Doig arranged for Raewyn and Graham to come and see them play in Wales. Doig tells of being confused when applause broke out prior to the match, when nothing was happening on the field. The clapping was for Henry as he walked to his seat. This type of adulation was difficult for Henry to deal with, knowing that the tide could turn just as quickly.

> **There is no doubt that the Welsh measure themselves against England. What happened was beyond their wildest dreams.**

In 1999 Wales started a purple patch. They won two test matches against the Pumas and enjoyed a memorable victory at Millennium Stadium against the Springboks, who had never lost to Wales before. This was a remarkable achievement, and led on to a run of eleven straight wins for the Welsh. In the wake of this success, Wales went to the 1999 World Cup full of confidence but were surprisingly beaten by the Samoans in pool play. They still topped their pool but were beaten by the Wallabies in the quarter-finals — the Wallabies going on to win the World Cup.

Throughout 2000 and 2001 the Welsh competed with some credit in the Six Nations championship but were unable to match it with England, who were far too strong for them.

It was against this background that Henry was offered the Lions job, and undoubtedly it influenced his decision. This was an honour, the only 'outsider' to be asked to coach the Home Nations and Ireland. Could he really do two fulltime jobs? He had made a good fist of being headmaster of Kelston Boys' High School while coaching Auckland — no small achievement. The world, or at least the Welsh part of it, was sure he could; and with that affirmation, he accepted.

From the outset, elements of the England team went out of their way to make things difficult for Henry. Clive Woodward was miffed he hadn't been given the job and the behaviour of two English players in particular, Austin Healey and Matt Dawson, was petulant, childish and selfish throughout the 2001 tour of Australia.

They did everything possible to undermine Henry and, ultimately, the Lions' effort to win the series. Many of the players on tour wrote newspaper columns, which in practice usually means they're ghost-written by media hacks looking for sensationalism. In my mind there is no question that this experience resulted in Henry ensuring that no All Black was involved in a similar enterprise in the 2007 World Cup year. Despite all these difficulties, the Lions nearly won the series. Rod Macqueen, coach of the Wallabies at the time, remembers the closeness and tension in the series.

'Graham Henry is a tough adversary. He is pragmatic, gritty and uncompromising — never willing to put a team out unprepared. There are never any obvious weaknesses in his teams. Most of all, he likes to win. The Lions v Australia series saw us both under a lot of pressure. Australia has always relied on a lot of preparation before a series, but for a variety of reasons we were limited to one hastily arranged game against the New Zealand Maori. On the other hand, the Lions were well prepared by seven pre-test fixtures.

'The decisive difference between the two squads was that the Aussies were close-knit, tight and loyal, while the Lions were full of players with their own agendas. We could see that there were a number of English players undermining the group and we made a deliberate decision to fuel this. In press statements and media statements we referred to the Lions as "the English team". I believed there was real animosity between Woodward and Henry, and felt that these elements were their Achilles heel.

'There was little between the two teams in terms of ability but when it came down to unity and loyalty they could not have been further apart. That was the difference . . . and that's why we won.'

At the end of the series Henry was lonely, dispirited, depressed and defeated. At no time in his life had he felt such emptiness. In hindsight, he was probably unwise to have accepted the Lions job while still coaching Wales — the combined workload was too great and he was compromised.

'The decisive difference between the two squads was that the Aussies were close-knit, tight and loyal, while the Lions were full of players with their own agendas.' — Wallabies coach Rod Macqueen

---

Unquestionably, if he'd been solely the Lions' coach he wouldn't have put up with the sniping of Dawson and Healey. Both would have been sent packing — but it wouldn't have been a good look for the coach of Wales to send home two English stars from a Lions tour. At the same time, the Welsh players in the Lions lost faith in him when he didn't pick them. Put bluntly, Henry had a conflict of interest and should never have accepted the Lions job without first relinquishing his Welsh commitments, an error of judgement that ultimately led to his resignation from Wales.

By November 2001, after defeats by the Wallabies and Argentina, Henry realized the end was near for him in Wales. If he had any doubts they quickly disappeared after a disastrous 54 – 10 loss to Ireland. He met with the Welsh authorities and had his contract terminated.

On the plus side, the Wales and Lions experiences turned Graham Henry from a very good coach into an excellent one. With both of those teams he was unable to rely on Polynesian flair or intuitive Kiwi rugby nous to pull them through. Instead he *coached* . . . passing, kicking, tackling, ball retention, backline alignments, simple game strategy and the essentials a provincial rugby coach in New Zealand can expect his players to have absorbed years before.

The Wales and Lions experiences turned Graham Henry from a very good coach into an excellent one.

Most of all he learnt how to deal with man-management, adulation and disappointment. In the first instance he had to get the Welsh players to believe in themselves, and believe they could win. This was no small task, given the sniping and criticism by former Welsh greats in print, on television and on radio. While Welsh rugby was stuck in a time warp somewhere between the late 1960s and early 1970s, Henry's big advantage was that he came from a country that hadn't been beaten by Wales since 1954. This is not to say he didn't respect J.P.R. Williams, Gareth Davies, Barry John and Gareth Edwards, but he wasn't prepared to rate their opinions as gospel thirty years on.

His independence, his objectivity, his diligence and, most of all, his loyalty to his players won them over, and the Welsh team became a solid unit. For this alone, to break from the shackles of the past,

Welsh rugby probably got him cheaply at a rumoured $750,000 per year.

The adulation was something Henry never sought. This is a quiet man, with a limited number of close friends, based in a foreign country without any real mates — and a nation wanting a piece of him. It was his best mate who put it firmly into perspective. Raewyn Henry refused to allow him to go to the supermarket with her, where shoppers queued up for autographs. Her pragmatism and earthy approach to life led to her exclaiming 'You're not a god . . . just a rugby coach.'

Henry arrived back in Auckland, where the ARU appointed him technical adviser. He was once again involved in the New Zealand rugby coaching system, but a much wiser man than he'd been prior to his Welsh experience. Auckland again went on to win Air New Zealand NPC titles in 2002 and 2003 with Henry involved, and he was a technical adviser for the Blues when they won the Super 12 in 2003.

By the time he returned to New Zealand, the 'Henry clause' had already been revoked, enabling former England assistant coach John Mitchell to take the position of All Black coach. At the time, the CEO of the NZRU, David Rutherford, told the NZPA: 'There are no issues relating to when he [Henry] left New Zealand. We reviewed the policy two years ago and removed it. There is no impediment. John Mitchell proves it.'

This change of direction by New Zealand rugby would also enable Henry to bring back Steve Hansen and Wayne Smith from the United Kingdom to make up his coaching panel.

The failure of the All Blacks to win the 2003 World Cup in Sydney led to a public outcry in New Zealand, demanding a change of coach. Not that John Mitchell had a bad record — on the surface it would appear as though Mitchell received harsh treatment. However, in the end the way Mitchell conducted himself with the media came back to haunt him when he failed to finish off the 'journey' he had promised to the New Zealand public.

Henry saw an opportunity and, using his typically thorough and painstaking approach, he rallied support, ideas and influence behind his bid to become the next All Black coach. His appointment was greeted with wide support and acclaim. He quickly gathered his management team around him, although not all appointments went his way.

Using his typically thorough and painstaking approach, Henry rallied support, ideas and influence behind his bid to become the next All Black coach.

He was keen to get Laurie Mains as a selector, but Mains had upset the NZRU in an employment dispute. Sir Brian Lochore was approached for the role, and accepted. Henry didn't achieve his first choice as backs coach either — Grant Fox declined, so Henry approached former All Black coach Wayne Smith, who at the time was coaching Northampton in England. Smith accepted. Henry had already had a brief working relationship with Steve Hansen who had been his assistant for a short time in Wales, and this connection led to Hansen's appointment as the forwards coach.

The scene was set for Henry to take on the ultimate prize of coaching the All Blacks. For the first time the coach would be one who had served a long apprenticeship, right through the grades. No other All Blacks coach had travelled such a journey. To say he was prepared and ready for the task was an understatement.

Any evaluation of Graham Henry's personality and character will ultimately concentrate on his focus, his single-mindedness and his steely determination. On occasions he can be charming, witty and interesting. After Henry's press conference announcing he was off to Wales, Paul Holmes remarked: 'He's a bloody good bloke. I'd always thought he was a boring bugger.'

At times he is. There is little balance in his life. In his defence, it is probably impossible for any All Black coach to lead a balanced life in New Zealand. Most of the country is besotted with rugby, talk it incessantly and desperately seek the inside oil from the All Black coach to share with mates.

> **It is probably impossible for any All Black coach to lead a balanced life in New Zealand. Most of the country is besotted with rugby.**

His old friend Chris Doig is right — Henry the over-achiever has made the very most of his abilities. His drive to succeed is matched only by his diligence. Nothing is left to chance. It is this insular single-mindedness that at times has left his mates feeling as if they've been walked over in a manner reminiscent of an All Black pack seeking the ball in a ruck. His goals are simple — to be the best coach he can possibly be, and coach of the best team in the world.

The one personality trait that continues to surprise is that of the gambler. It is shown in the selections of unknowns like Kaino and Toeava, in game plans like the famous defeat of Canterbury in 1995 and in his support for Troy Flavell. Yet the gambles are calculated, cleverly assessed and accurately put into play.

> The one personality trait that continues to surprise is that of the gambler. Yet the gambles are calculated, cleverly assessed and accurately put into play.

No other coach has served such an apprenticeship — from schoolboys at Auckland Grammar right through to taking charge of the All Blacks. Though it could hardly make them forget the disappointment of recent World Cups, All Black supporters could at least go into the 2007 World Cup confident that, in Graham Henry, they had the best man available leading them into battle.

The Captain

'McCaw is an exceptional flanker with a fantastic work rate and a great understanding of the modern game. He continues to develop as a captain and will always be someone who leads from the front.'
— Wayne Shelford

- Is he the best openside flanker of all time?

- Is he a cheat?

- Can a great player make a great leader?

WHEN GRAHAM HENRY took over as All Black coach and addressed his long-term goal of winning the World Cup in 2007, he only needed to look back in the history books to realize that his on-field leader was one of the most crucial choices he would make. The five World Cup winning captains — David Kirk, Nick Farr-Jones, Francois Pienaar, John Eales and Martin Johnson — were all respected as rugby players before they led their teams to glory in the World Cup. For Henry the challenge was to find someone within his squad who could match these five renowned players' standing in the game.

Initially there was no clear-cut choice. Waiting in the wings was the young Richie McCaw, seen by many to already have some leadership qualities. But at the time Henry took over, McCaw was busy cementing his position in the All Blacks and hadn't even captained his Canterbury provincial side.

Thorne became known as the 'invisible man' by many rugby fans and some media because he was so rarely spotted getting involved in the game.

A change of captain was inevitable and necessary, though, because if one thing stood out about New Zealand's unsuccessful campaign in 2003 it was the doubt many people had about captain Reuben Thorne's playing ability. Doubts about his ability to lead the All Blacks had also been consistently raised — most commonly as an extension of people's doubts over whether he deserved to make the team as a player. Thorne had become known as the 'invisible man' by many rugby fans and some media because he was so rarely spotted getting involved in the game. His supporters, who largely came from the Canterbury region, argued strongly that he was often not seen on the field because — unlike other, flashier players — he was prepared to do the 'dirty work' so that others, particularly his fellow loose forwards, could flourish.

Henry's choice of his first captain couldn't have been better. By choosing Tana Umaga he was able to unite the All Black players and fans. The trust between Henry and Umaga was tested early on as the new captain held on to the secret of his appointment for two months before the news was finally made public, with the announcement of two All Black trial teams.

Leading Umaga's list of attributes was that he was seen as a certain pick by his fellow players, the coaching staff and the New Zealand public. However, there was more to it than that. Umaga possessed charisma and a passion for rugby similar to that which Buck Shelford displayed back in the 1980s, during his leadership of the All Blacks. Umaga was the first Samoan to captain the All Blacks, and the fact that he was a Pacific Islander was a bonus for Henry. Umaga added a Polynesian flavour to what might otherwise have been perceived as a white, middle-aged management group.

Tana's role should never be underestimated in the totality of Henry's World Cup campaign. His selection was such a success that if it hadn't been for him losing his passion for the game, Henry would undoubtedly have stuck by him as captain right through to the World Cup. Even when Tana made up his mind to retire, Henry made every effort to encourage him to remain in the game. Suggestions such as cutting his travel and test demands and even taking a gap year were made, but were all turned down by Umaga.

Tana's role should never be underestimated in the totality of Henry's World Cup campaign.

I have no doubt that the fallout from Umaga and Mealamu's controversial tackle on Lions captain Brian O'Driscoll in 2005 played a large role in Tana wanting to escape from international rugby when he did. Not only did the strain take its toll, but it also placed extreme pressure on his family. This continued right through the end-of-year tour to Europe, where media scrutiny and even alleged death threats helped to strengthen his conviction to retire.

In losing Umaga, Henry not only lost his captain but one of his best men. Despite his talented pool of players, he would struggle to find a permanent replacement midfielder for Umaga right up to the World Cup.

Umaga's replacement as captain was an easy decision. Along with the rest of his management team, Henry had identified in McCaw all the attributes required to lead his team. By the time Umaga's successor was named, McCaw was two years wiser, had already been given two tests in charge of the team and, even though he was still only twenty-five, he was undoubtedly at the peak of his powers as a player.

It surprises many people to learn that when McCaw was coming through the grades he hadn't been used as a captain as much as people might presume. In Kurow as a boy, his coach had spread the duties around every week, and although he was the head boy and runner-up to dux at Otago Boys' High School, he never led the first fifteen. In fact, since taking over the role, McCaw has confessed that captaining the All Blacks was never something he dreamed of as a kid. 'When I was young I used to dream about running around with the silver fern on, but as a young fellow the thought of being captain never crossed my mind.'

It surprises many people to learn that when McCaw was coming through the grades he hadn't been used as a captain as much as people might presume.

McCaw became prominent as a leader when he filled in for squad captain Aaron Mauger as captain of the victorious New Zealand Under 21 side in the final of the 2001 Under 21 championship. By the time he took over the All Black job properly in 2006 he'd also captained the 2004 and 2005 Canterbury NPC sides to victory, as well as the Super-12-winning 2005 Crusaders. In addition, he had also served as the vice-captain of the All Blacks under Tana Umaga for the previous two years.

Back in 2004, concern had been voiced over his ability to lead after his career was threatened by head injuries which kept him out of the middle part of the season. His first test as All Black captain came against Wales in 2004, and nearly turned into a nightmare as the All Blacks just got out of jail to win 26 – 25 against a fired-up Welsh side. After the match McCaw expressed how happy he was to get away with a win. 'I guess there's a bit of relief, which is usual after a game like that, but pleasure as well, because the guys had to dig deep. There's a lot of young guys that probably haven't experienced a test match like that before, and to come out the right side of it, I was so pleased for all those guys.'

The other test he captained prior to taking over the captaincy on a fulltime basis was during the end-of-year tour the following year against Ireland. This time the 45 – 7 victory came much more easily, and McCaw was one of the standout players in the All Blacks' easy victory.

When Henry finally got round to officially announcing McCaw as the successor to Umaga, he was the first to acknowledge it had been an easy decision — succession planning was alive and well within the All Black camp. 'It's a natural step for Richie McCaw to take on the captain's role. He has been an All Black since 2001, he is a world-class player, and he has led the team well in previous tests. He has also been a highly successful captain with the Crusaders and with Canterbury,' said Henry.

The one doubt many people had about McCaw as captain was that it might be risky for such a valuable player. The burden of captaincy has affected the performance of many cricketers over the years. Maybe the same could happen to McCaw?

Those concerns were soon forgotten as McCaw grew as a leader during the 2005 season, playing as captain of the Crusaders. It appeared the captaincy made him want to lift his game to even greater heights, possibly to prove a point to anyone who doubted his ability to perform the dual roles of player and captain.

Henry's selection of Jerry Collins ahead of someone like Anton Oliver, with much more leadership experience, merely confirmed how intent he was on moving on from the mistakes of the past.

Probably the biggest surprise regarding McCaw's fulltime captaincy of the men in black came in 2006 with the announcement of his vice-captain, Jerry Collins. It was to be an important appointment in the 'Henry era' due to the rotation of players, but was even more significant due to Henry's decision in 2006 to operate a split-squad system for the early test matches. This meant Collins captained the third test of the year against Argentina, with McCaw left at home to rest up for the extended Tri-Nations series. Collins had leadership experience on a national level, having captained the New Zealand schools' side. In 1999, at age eighteen, he had been one of the youngest players in the world to captain a senior club team when he led Northern United.

Henry's selection of Collins ahead of someone like Anton Oliver, with much more leadership experience, merely confirmed how intent he was on moving on from the mistakes of the past. Collins had become one of about five certainties for any All Black top team — and for Henry, that was the most important leadership prerequisite. Ironically Collins had made the number 6 jersey his own after so much doubt had surrounded it when it had been worn by Reuben Thorne.

Captaincy has changed in the modern game, with a wider leadership group including coaches and senior management now having a significant input. McCaw is the first to acknowledge that key members of the team are valuable in aiding his decision making. 'You have to make sure everyone contributes the experience they have got in the team. You have to use everyone. That's the strength of the good captains I have been involved with, encouraging others to have their ideas.'

McCaw's consistently high standard of play throughout the 2006 season quickly put to rest any remaining doubts about the burden of the All Black captaincy negatively affecting his game. Henry's faith in his captain was rewarded on the field with eleven wins from the twelve tests he played that year. Henry and McCaw both identified a lack of hunger in the All Blacks for the one loss against South Africa in Rustenburg, although nobody could criticize McCaw for his performance that day, which was right out of the top drawer.

At the end of 2006 his consistently high standard of play was recognized when McCaw won the 2006 International Rugby Players' Association Player of the Year and the IRB World Player of the Year awards, as well as top New Zealand sportsperson at the People's Choice Sports Awards.

A possible injury to McCaw remained one of the few concerns for All Black fans going into World Cup year.

Henry showed a reluctance to rest his captain right through the 2006 season, apart from the test in Argentina. This was a surprise to many people, considering how much the openside flanker's body is bashed around in the modern game. A possible injury to McCaw remained one of the few concerns for All Black fans going into World Cup year, as they questioned just how much the team would suffer if he was badly injured before or during the World Cup.

There was no shortage of back-ups. Fans agreed Marty Holah and Josh Blackie would walk into most international teams; and the player recognized by the selection panel as McCaw's replacement, Chris Masoe, continued to show progress as an international player. It was therefore surprising that Masoe wasn't given more test experience during 2006, alongside Jerry Collins and Rodney So'oialo.

Henry's reliance on Richie McCaw, along with Dan Carter, came into question following the 2006 Tri-Nations series, when some critics felt he became over-sensitive about the treatment his two star players were receiving from opposition teams. Henry even went as far as to say he'd complain to the IRB about the judicial system's inability to deal with incidents of foul play. The most notable of these occurred in the Eden Park test against Australia that August, when Lote Tuqiri received a ten-week suspension for a spear tackle on McCaw and a high-swinging arm from Phil Waugh broke the All Black captain's nose. 'There have been some incidents in international rugby this year that I think shouldn't be in rugby,' Henry said. 'I intend to talk to the IRB about that. That's the right channel.'

When questioned about Henry's comments, Wallaby coach John Connolly hit back, highlighting the fact that McCaw was such a dangerous opponent that all teams — including New Zealand ones — would attempt to put him off his game as best they could. It was a valid point. 'All you have to do is drag out a tape of a Hurricanes–Crusaders Super 14 match, and watch Jerry Collins and Richie McCaw go hammer and tongs at each other. And I didn't see any criticism of Collins after those games.'

McCaw in 2006 was such a dangerous opponent that all teams — including New Zealand ones — would attempt to put him off his game as best they could.

Support for 'Knuckles' Connolly's case can indeed be found from within matches played by New Zealand teams against McCaw. In the 2006 round-robin clash between the Crusaders and Hurricanes, the Wellington-based franchise singled McCaw out for special attention. At one breakdown, Hurricanes back-rower Jerry Collins hurled the ball at McCaw's head in frustration after the referee had blown a penalty. Prop Neemia Tialata was later caught on camera blatantly trying to throttle McCaw at the bottom of a ruck.

People who professed to be 'in the know' called talkback radio expressing the view that some of the Hurricanes players felt McCaw had been responsible for part of the pressure that led to Tana Umaga retiring as captain. The argument was that this was them getting back at him. Attempts to establish whether there was any truth in this understandably met a black brick wall.

If you ask me, in McCaw's case I think there did seem to be a vindictive nastiness permeating the actions of the Hurricanes players. Nick Farr-Jones is on record outlining that a key strategy when his Wallabies team took on the All Blacks was to try to keep key flanker Michael Jones at the bottom of as many rucks as possible.

Connolly let his own frustration get the better of him when further discussing McCaw. 'Referees do have to watch all this closely because teams get frustrated because he [McCaw] is so often offside. He takes off from the scrum early, and continually rolls over the ball. So there's a huge onus on the referees.'

Part of what Connolly says is true. Many good loose forwards are cheats. McCaw is the best in the business. Does this also make him the best cheat? For example, he rarely leaves the scrum early, he's far too screwed-on for that — and Connolly should know it. However, in his quest to be first to the breakdown McCaw can often become isolated and appear offside. To make matters even more difficult, at this convoluted point in the evolution of the game no one, including McCaw, Connolly, the referee, the writer or the reader, has the faintest idea what is legal and what is illegal at the breakdown. In reality indecision, doubt, dispute and interpretation of the law in this area have turned rugby from a game into something more akin to a puzzle. In such an environment a player as good as McCaw is always going to be subjected to accusations like those made by Connolly.

The reality is that when those accusations cease, it will be a sure sign that Richie McCaw is no longer playing well.

Leading into the 2007 season, McCaw was one player who relished the conditioning window Henry created for twenty-two of his key players. He enjoyed the mental relief as much as anything during the conditioning period, and said as much at the time. 'The thing you can't underestimate is the mental freshness of the guys. I'm sure there are guys perhaps watching the games who wish they were out playing, but having weekends free after a hard week of training is something a wee bit unique. And to be able to relax and do a few things that you want to do is something great. I know personally you get the enthusiasm back to play again because you've had this time.'

When he finally returned to the field, however, his form was average by his own high standards, and like many of the other conditioned All Blacks he struggled to get back to his best form before the Super 14 competition finished.

His first match back was notable for the way he was targeted by the Stormers at Jade Stadium. Within the first fifteen minutes there had been a series of cheap shots aimed at him. One errant elbow by Schalk Burger was an indication of what McCaw might have to deal with during the tests later in the year. Equally as concerning was the lack of action by the referee to protect McCaw and punish the perpetrators.

> Ten minutes in the bin in a key match could easily translate into losing the World Cup for the All Blacks.

This frustrating period for McCaw showed through in the rare lack of discipline he displayed when he was yellow-carded twice in the later part of the competition. Whether he was guilty or not was irrelevant — his lack of judgement and unwillingness to heed the warnings of the referees were a serious concern. Ten minutes in the bin in a key match could easily translate into losing the World Cup for the All Blacks.

Come test time Henry resisted the temptation to rest his captain for the two tests against France. However, he did give Chris Masoe some game time and even started him against Canada. The general feeling from most critics was that Henry was taking a real risk by not giving a player like Marty Holah more time in the All Black camp, just in case McCaw received a major injury. But even though McCaw wasn't at the top of his own game, he once again showed what a difference he made when he was on the park during the tests leading up to the Tri-Nations.

By the time the 2007 Tri-Nations arrived, McCaw was beginning to look like his old self. He played every minute of every game, once more highlighting Henry's reliance on his captain. Considering he plays in the most high-risk position in the modern game, it is staggering that he gets so few spells. It suggests strongly to me that Henry does not believe he can win if Richie isn't on the field. This makes it more remarkable that a second specialist openside flanker wasn't selected for the World Cup squad — in my opinion a huge gamble on the part of Henry and his fellow selectors.

McCaw remains contracted to the NZRU until the end of 2007;

however, on 13 June he gave an indication that he is committed to staying in New Zealand longer than that by signing a deal to become an 'ambassador' for Westpac Bank. McCaw said his two-year arrangement with the bank 'definitely will' help him stay in this country. Every New Zealand rugby supporter will hope that this is the case, and that McCaw sticks around until 2011 to help New Zealand win the World Cup on home soil.

The Star

'We have been blessed with some special first-fives over the years . . . But I've no doubt Carter is going to be the greatest we've ever had.' — Grant Fox

- Is he the greatest All Black of all time?

- Would he have come through the Auckland system up against bigger Polynesian players?

- How can he model undies and still keep his feet on the ground?

At only twenty-six, Dan Carter has already been described by many critics as a better player than any other first-five the All Blacks have produced. One of the 'greats' Carter has already leap-frogged over is Grant Fox, himself now a respected rugby critic. While all five previous World-Cup-winning coaches have had strong captains to work with, they have also had world-class first-fives integral in guiding their teams to victory. Sir Brian Lochore had Grant Fox in 1987 — the top points-scorer for the tournament and, just as importantly, able to guide the All Blacks around the park with poise and precision.

In 1991 Bob Dwyer had Michael Lynagh as his number 10; he remains the greatest points-scorer in Australian rugby history. His try in the dying minutes of Australia's quarter-final at the 1991 World Cup broke the hearts of the Irish who were leading 18 – 15 up to that point.

In 1995 South African coach Kitch Christie put Joel Stransky in the number 10 jersey; he proceeded to write himself into the history books by kicking the drop-goal which won the Springboks the match in extra time.

Rod Macqueen converted Stephen Larkham from a promising fullback into one of the greatest first-fives Australian rugby has produced. Larkham's value to him at the 1999 World Cup was never more evident than when he kicked the drop-goal to win the semi-final match against South Africa in extra time.

History signalled loud and clear to Graham Henry that one of the most important jobs on his list was to find a world-class number 10 to help him win the 2007 World Cup.

And we all know what happened in 2003 — even though we'd rather forget. Clive Woodward didn't have the same level of talent John Mitchell had throughout his All Black squad that year, but in Jonny Wilkinson he had a play-maker able to take advantage of England's massive, dominant forward pack. England wouldn't have got close to winning the Cup without him, but with him, they captured victory in the final minutes of extra time courtesy of Wilkinson's drop-goal.

History signalled loud and clear to Graham Henry that one of the most important jobs on his list was to find a world-class number 10 to help him win the 2007 World Cup. If Henry could have been granted one wish, he would have wished for a player that walked, talked and played rugby like Dan Carter.

Even with Henry's great eye for talent, he would have struggled to predict that the young Dan Carter, at age twenty-one predominantly a second five-eighth, would turn into one of the greatest players New Zealand rugby has produced. By the end of 2007, however, Carter would prove himself to be the world-class number 10 Henry needed.

Graham Henry has been lucky to have some very talented players play under him, but no one has ever been as complete as Dan Carter. Carter simply has everything — speed, agility, a brilliant kicking game, a crisp pass, a lovely fend and, most importantly, a cool rugby brain.

Two things stand out about Carter. First, he has the asset that all great sportsmen tend to have — time. Yet for all Carter's natural ability, he also has the work ethic to back it up. Because of this, he is able not only to be consistent with his performances but is also constantly improving.

When you look back on his career so far, the amazing things about Carter are that the New Zealand rugby system took so long to identify him and, when he *was* noticed, how sharp his rise through the ranks was.

Coincidentally, Dan Carter's rise to fame began back in his

seventh-form year, when he became a boarder at Graham Henry's old school — Christchurch Boys' High School. The move came as a result of the exposure Carter gained following selection in a Canterbury schools' side the previous year. Up until then 'D.C.' had remained a hidden talent, living in the small town of Southbridge and attending his local secondary school, Ellesmere College.

Would Carter have survived in an environment like the Auckland secondary school system, which is dominated by physically mature Polynesian boys?

It may seem unusual that in the era of professional rugby, when scouts seem to be everywhere, Carter could remain under wraps for so long. One explanation that helps to make slightly more sense of this is that, physically, Carter was a late developer. One question this raises is whether Carter would have survived in an environment like the Auckland secondary school system, which is dominated by physically mature Polynesian boys. Kelston Boys' High School, where Henry was principal for many years, is a prime example of this: big Polynesian boys make up the bulk of their first fifteen teams. Soccer would have been a much more appropriate and safer sport for someone the size of the young Dan Carter at secondary school.

In reality Carter's rugby heritage may have been strong enough to lead him towards rugby, wherever he was raised. His father Neville represented Canterbury County at centre and fullback, and was just one of many of the extended Carter family to have played the oval ball with some distinction.

For much of his teenage years, Carter's small stature meant he played halfback. Considering he played most of his early NPC and Super rugby as a second five-eighth, it remains all the more stunning how well Carter took to the All Black first five-eighth role when Henry moved him there for the United Kingdom trip at the end of 2004.

It is a credit not only to himself, but to all his coaches, just how quickly Carter has progressed since 2002, when he first played for Canterbury. Both Henry and Robbie Deans, Carter's other predominant coach since then, have been at pains to point out the preparation Carter puts in off the field. He is a coach's dream. In many ways the best coaching Deans and Henry have been able to give Carter is to not coach him at all.

In hindsight, Henry may have been half a season slow in moving Carter from second-five to first-five. Like many coaches, Henry stuck with a man who had done the job for him in the past. This meant Carlos Spencer spent most of the 2004 Tri-Nations in the number 10 jersey while Carter remained at number 12, the position John Mitchell had also preferred to use him in early in his career.

In hindsight, Henry may have been half a season slow in moving Carter from second-five to first-five.

The way Spencer under-performed that year during the Tri-Nations and the way Carter took to the job so smoothly on the end-of-year tour leaves you with the feeling that South Africa's victory in the 2004 Tri-Nations could have been avoided had Carter been placed in the pivotal role earlier. For Henry, it was a case of better late than never. The end-of-year tour to the UK presented him with a grand opportunity to experiment with some selections, and Carter at first-five quickly shaped up as the most important of these.

Two notable exclusions from the squad to tour Europe in November and December 2004 were Carlos Spencer and Andrew Mehrtens. It was a clear statement by Henry that it was time to move on and discover who he could use at first-five at the 2007 World Cup. Despite the compelling form displayed by Carter, Henry had intended to use Luke McAlister in the last match of this tour against the Barbarians; however, a recurrence of his hamstring injury put an end to this plan and Aaron Mauger stepped into first-five for the match.

In 2005 Carter was used for the first time as the first-choice first-five for the Crusaders throughout a Super 12 campaign. He quickly made himself at home in the position, and one of the much-awaited clashes of the 2005 season became his head-to-head battle with Lions star player Jonny Wilkinson. Much like Henry's convincing victory over Clive Woodward, Carter's was a one-horse race as D.C. wrote himself into the record books.

In the All Blacks' 48 – 18 second test win against the Lions, Carter accumulated a personal tally of 32 points, courtesy of two tries and nine out of ten successful goal attempts. It was not so much about the points, though — it was more the *way* he played that had people in raptures. He was so outstanding in the series that everyone — from fans to ex-players to the media — began asking whether he was not just the greatest current player, but the greatest player of all time.

Back in England, Michael Auglin, writing for the *Observer*, said:

> Roger Federer has been described as the greatest tennis player largely because, even though he is merely 23 and learning, he does not appear to have a weakness. And here in New Zealand, where some of the most respected rugby writers are plying their trade, Daniel Carter has had the same treatment for the same reason. There does not seem to be a weakness in his game.

In his *Sunday Star Times* column, the usually conservative Grant Fox wrote:

> As with everyone last night I found it difficult to find enough superlatives for Daniel Carter, who was the undoubted star of the 48 – 18 second test win . . . We have been blessed with some special first-fives over the years . . . But I've no doubt Carter is going to be the greatest we've had.

Former All Black captain David Kirk chipped in this year by pronouncing in a radio interview:

> It is very difficult to compare across generations and positions, but Dan Carter is the best first-five I have seen. In the second test against the Lions he was sublime.

Carter's goalkicking was one skill that took a big leap forward in the 2005 season. He had been used in the role for the All Blacks even when he was playing second-five, but in 2005 his consistency went up a notch, making him even more accurate.

The biggest concern for All Black supporters quickly became whether the All Blacks under Graham Henry were too reliant on Carter. What would they do if he was injured before or during the World Cup? A preview of that prospect came in the third Lions test, when Carter was unable to play due to a shoulder injury. Initially Leon MacDonald was the preferred back-up, but he was ruled out the Wednesday of the match with a groin injury. Next in line was Luke McAlister, who performed with distinction as Carter's replacement, with Nick Evans sitting on the bench that day as a further back-up.

The frightening prospect of life without Carter was again brought home to Henry during the 2005 Tri-Nations campaign, when Carter broke his leg in the All Blacks 30 – 13 win over Australia in Sydney. Once again Leon MacDonald was used as the first-five replacement for the two remaining tests. This proved to be a poor choice by the All Black selection panel, with no real progress made towards a long-term back-up for Carter. The only thing that was confirmed was that MacDonald was not a viable replacement, having had his kicks charged down for important tries two weeks in a row.

Right throughout 2006, Carter's possible replacements continued to be given minimal game time and, apart from the first two tests of the year, Carter started every test.

Nick Evans was given a couple of opportunities to start in the number 10 jersey on the end-of-year tour, and showed he had potential to become Carter's back-up for the World Cup. However, right throughout 2006 Carter's possible replacements continued to be given minimal game time and, apart from the first two tests of the year, where he was rested completely, Carter started every test.

Admittedly it didn't help the All Black coaching staff's planning that Evans was out of contention for the first half of 2006 following shoulder surgery. McAlister then became the logical choice for the first two tests of the year when the decision to rest Carter had been made. With no Evans to call upon, the lack of replacement top first-fives was exposed when David Hill was called up to the 22 for both tests, making his test debut from the bench.

Carter produced one of the standout moments of the 2006 All Black season when he kicked a 61-metre penalty goal just before halftime in the 45 – 26 win over South Africa. It remains one of the longest successful penalty kicks by an All Black of all time. A delightful story emerged after the match, which highlights the spirit that makes this All Black team tick. When the penalty was awarded, Carter was unsure. Luke McAlister came up to him and said, 'Go on, D.C. Have a go. You're all over it, mate.'

Carter was again at the top of his game on the end-of-year tour, accumulating 72 points in four matches. It remains surprising, however, that Evans wasn't given more game time, with Carter starting all the matches.

With Carter's career needing to peak in 2007, the conditioning period appeared to hamper his momentum. He struggled with his entry into Super 14 rugby, like so many of his team-mates who also sat out the first half of the competition. In part his return was hampered by a niggling neck injury that at one stage threatened to keep him out of the Crusaders semi-final against the Bulls. While he did play the match, he failed to make the same impact he had previously on other crucial matches during his short but illustrious career.

With Carter's career needing to peak in 2007, the conditioning period appeared to hamper his momentum.

Come test time, injury again hampered Carter and he was replaced at halftime in the first test of the year, against France. He missed the following match and, despite a three-try haul next against Canada, confessed after that match that he needed to lift his game for the Tri-Nations to come.

D.C. had a patchy Tri-Nations series. He appeared to be struggling for form, and when he came back looked to be carrying an injury.

Fans were quick to point out that he had only a shadow of his previous form, but when questioned at the end of the Tri-Nations, the astute Robbie Deans said Carter's form had never concerned him. Deans added that it was what was happening *around* Carter that had affected the star's form. In the final Tri-Nations match on a wet Eden Park, once again it was the deadly accurate boot of Dan Carter that led to the All Blacks winning both the Bledisloe Cup and the Tri-Nations.

Carter has been able to keep his feet on the ground when it could have been so easy for him to get caught up in the unprecedented adulation he receives within New Zealand. Not only are most New Zealand men in awe of Carter, but the women have also fallen in love with his devastating combination of handsome looks and quietly spoken demeanour.

Carter is a very marketable product, but thankfully for Henry he hasn't been over-exposed — a tribute not only to Carter himself but also to the people with whom he has surrounded himself, within both the All Blacks and his Canterbury teams. His marketing manager, Dean Hegan, suggested earlier this year that World Cup victory would be of huge financial significance to Carter, adding inestimable value to his brand, saying, 'You'd be naïve to think that it wouldn't impact on his commercial value.'

> **Carter is a very marketable product, but thankfully for Henry he hasn't been over-exposed.**

Being part of the All Black team at the World Cup opens up new opportunities for Carter. Jonah Lomu's individual performances at the 1995 and 1999 World Cups made him a household name around the world, despite the All Blacks' failure to win both titles. The NZRU's own link to major commercial companies heavily restricts the options available to players like Carter, which is why major deals like the one he has with Jockey are so valuable. Carter himself is mindful of keeping his priorities clearly sorted, saying that he still sees himself as a rugby player. 'My main focus is to always keep it that way, to make sure people see me for a rugby player first and a brand second.'

When questioned about the dangers of getting a swelled head from all the publicity, Carter consistently refers back to his close friends and family, who keep him grounded. In saying that, if Carter ever did start to lose his way, you can guarantee Henry would be quick to kick him back into shape.

Henry can be thankful Carter is equally determined to win the 2007 World Cup. While rumours have come and gone of other players' plans to head overseas, the key play-maker within Henry's team never raised an eyebrow at the type of money he could earn overseas. He has acknowledged that, like his predecessors, the temptation of combining travel with the ability to earn good money could be something to indulge in later in his career. In the meantime the New Zealand public will no doubt pray that somewhere in the NZRU treasure chest there is a significantly generous 'Dan Carter allowance'.

Henry can be thankful Carter is equally determined to win the 2007 World Cup.

While Carter has never been one to be controlled by money, he is only human, and the way he plays rugby you'd have to think that any money put aside for keeping him in the black jersey through to 2011 would be money well spent.

The Squad

Few All Black coaches have had such talent to pick from, and it can be argued that this talent base is the most positive result of rotation. The challenge was to coordinate that talent into a World Cup-winning team.

- Was this a group of champions or a champion team?

- Has a replacement for Tana Umaga been found as a player and a leader?

- Was the balance of the squad right?

JERRY COLLINS

Can a gladiator have a good heart?

If Hollywood had known about Jerry Collins, Russell Crowe would never have won an Oscar for his role in *The Gladiator*. Jerry could have played the part without acting — *and* filled in as Schwarzenegger's double in a *Terminator* sequel during his spare time.

There was a constant cry some years ago for the 'mongrel' to come back into All Black forward play. Fans referred to the legends of the past, like 'Cowboy' Shaw and Buck Shelford, who were able to intimidate opposition teams with their ruthless win-at-all-costs attitude. Since Jerry Collins' arrival, those calls have been silenced.

Collins tackles with a brutality unmatched by any other modern player. What a shame that the phrase 'He has no respect for his body' is now a cliché . . . it should have been exclusively reserved for Jerry Collins.

There was a time early in his career when Jerry was viewed as a one-dimensional player with the ball in hand, because he rarely looked to pass or offload. In recent times he has broadened his game to include effective offloads, good passes and deft grubber kicks.

Collins tackles with a brutality unmatched by any other modern player.

Collins looks much more comfortable on the blindside flank than at number 8, where he was used by John Mitchell. Graham Henry reverted to trying Jerry at the back of the scrum in the second test against France in 2007, and the bulldozer looked as if it had run out of diesel. Perhaps Collins was understandably confused, not only by this selection, but also by Reuben Thorne being made captain ahead of him for that test. After all, Collins had been signalled as next-in-line after McCaw in 2006 when he was appointed captain for the tests against Argentina. No adequate public explanation was given by Henry at the time.

On the field Collins may be intimidating, yet off the field it's Jerry the Joker. All sorts of people like him and he has a reputation for being hard-case. Some even claim he's a mummy's boy who often talks about buying his mum a house from his rugby income. A few have said he's a big softy — but not too loudly.

Jerry is rapidly becoming a cult hero. He has enjoyed special popularity in Wellington, based on his loyalty to his beloved Northern United club, whose senior team he captained while still only eighteen. He hasn't been a fan of player rotation and prefers to play club rugby at times when most of his All Black team-mates have been resting. These actions have suggested to the public that he is 'one of them', and has further endeared him to the grass roots fans.

On the field Collins may be intimidating, yet off the field it's Jerry the Joker.

His popularity was tested in 2006 when Collins was caught by a television camera urinating on the Jade Stadium surface, moments before the start of the home Bledisloe test. He certainly wasn't the first to do it; nor will he be the last. The only thing that made this any different from other 'calls of nature' was it was caught on television. Collins' growing popularity survived the incident — and may even have been enhanced by it in some quarters.

Collins is playing better now than ever before. His true value to the All Blacks only seems to become apparent when they leave him on the bench. He was without doubt one of Henry's key players going into the World Cup and, like Carter and McCaw, he was irreplaceable.

ANDREW ELLIS

Living proof that even a master plan may need last-minute tweaking.

Andrew Ellis was the biggest surprise in the All Blacks 2007 World Cup squad. Right up till the naming of the squad it appeared that Piri Weepu had the third halfback position sewn up.

Just why the selectors changed their minds as dramatically as they did will remain a mystery.

Ellis's selection amounted to a massive turnaround for Graham Henry and his fellow selectors. On gaining selection, Ellis revealed he'd had no contact with them all season. In contrast, the All Black selectors had given Weepu permission to play first-five for the Hurricanes earlier in the season, which appeared to indicate his position in the squad was safe. Henry even waxed lyrical about his first performance there: 'Piri was outstanding on Friday night. Piri showing he can play there is a bonus for us. If we do have a problem, or when we come to pick a 22-man squad, we could have one number 10 and two halfbacks but know he could play there and play there very well.'

Just why the selectors changed their minds as dramatically as they did will remain a mystery, though if Henry's word is to be taken literally it was solely a decision 'based on form'. It completed a year of fluctuating fortunes for Ellis. In 2006 he was picked for the team and played a total of 20 minutes off the bench in the England and France test matches; in 2007 Ellis appeared to be out of favour after some average Super 14 form. When he announced the World Cup squad, Henry said it was with the Juniors that Ellis had shown sufficient form to play his way into the team. No one at that press conference, or in any of the innumerable columns that followed, believed him. In the first instance, the Juniors played such hopeless opposition it was difficult to judge whether a player was on top of his game; and second, Ellis played no better than the other halfback with the Juniors, Jimmy Cowan. Most speculated that Weepu's loss of form and some attitudinal problems led to him being dropped. Ellis was the player to benefit.

NICK EVANS

What might Evans have achieved if his career hadn't clashed with Carter's?

Nick Evans' career has suffered due to both his 'utility' tag and his injury-prone nature, and I get the feeling that because of these factors, the best may be yet to come from him. While Evans is now given the crucial tag of 'Dan Carter's back-up', it was as fullback that he started his first two tests for the All Blacks during the 2004 season.

> The reluctance to use Evans was confusing, considering that when he was given opportunities he performed.

Evans has always preferred first-five, and his move to the Highlanders for the 2004 season eventually gave him the game time in that position at Super 14 level to prove how valuable he can be there at national level. Unfortunately, Graham Henry's reluctance to rest Dan Carter meant that going into the 2007 World Cup, Evans' game time for the All Blacks had been very limited.

The reluctance to use him was confusing, considering that when he was given opportunities he performed. A prime example came in the Welsh test at the end of 2006 when he came on with less than 20 minutes to go — and broke the line with his first touch of the ball to set up a try. With the All Blacks up by 25 points at halftime, this was the type of situation Evans could have been used in to get a solid half of test rugby in the fly-half position behind him.

Evans' ability to play fullback was also overlooked by the selectors, something acknowledged by assistant coach Wayne Smith following the 2007 defeat in Melbourne. 'Obviously, we've got to look at that a lot more seriously and give Nick some game time at fullback. He'll probably cover that position off the bench if he's not starting.'

No player in New Zealand rugby appears to punt the ball as far as Evans. He primarily uses the drop-punt, a skill he developed over many years playing Australian Rules. In that code he represented New Zealand at Under 21 and senior level and was offered a trial by the Sydney Swans.

The most appealing aspect of Evans' game is his explosive, deceptive acceleration. He has suffered in recent years from playing in Otago and Highlander teams devoid of talented backs able to utilize the opportunities he creates.

> Ironically Evans probably possesses more leadership qualities and intelligence than most of the other players.

Evans is a bright, engaging personality who brings vision to the game. In an environment where team management would like you to believe every second player is a 'leader', the tag is never given to him. Ironically he probably possesses more leadership qualities and intelligence than most of the others. Unfortunately he won't get a chance to lead because he is likely to remain in Carter's shadow.

What Evans decides for his own future after the World Cup will be very important. He made it clear in May 2007 that he was returning home to live in Auckland. A few months later, his signing with Auckland was a disappointment for his former Harbour province but a coup for the Blues franchise, which had struggled to fill the number 10 jersey since Carlos Spencer's departure overseas.

New Zealand rugby was lucky not to lose Evans. Despite not being a first-stringer, you have to suspect he would be a player whose true value to the All Blacks won't be realized until he's gone.

CARL HAYMAN

Is he really the best prop in the world?

It may be a much abused cliché, but it's true: to win a rugby match you first have to win the contest up-front. That explains why many people have viewed Carl Hayman as the most valuable player in the All Blacks in recent times.

He is widely regarded as the most devastating scrummager of his generation, with Graham Henry on record acknowledging Hayman as the 'best tighthead in the world and an outstanding team man'. He is tall for a prop and has been rated by former All Black coach Laurie Mains as the best lineout support player in the business. Together with hooker Anton Oliver and loosehead prop Clarke Dermody, Carl Hayman has given the Highlanders a strong foundation in recent seasons. The poor performances of the southern franchise over the past three years would suggest there is now more to winning rugby matches than scrummaging well.

Hayman is widely regarded as the most devastating scrummager of his generation.

However, the NZRU obviously believes it is still important. The union did everything possible to try to keep Hayman in New Zealand after the last World Cup. As Deputy CEO Steve Tew explained, 'We put the very best possible offer in front of Carl and we are grateful that he gave it serious consideration.' The rumour mill suggested that the NZRU had offered to fund Hayman into a farm and had matched the Newcastle Falcons offer, reputed to be $1 million a year.

Graham Henry probably got closer to it than anyone else when he said, 'I think Carl would like to get out of the international spotlight for a while and sees this move as the best way to extend his time in the game.' Reports from people close to Hayman in Dunedin went further, suggesting he was tired and wanted a change of scene. The big man himself wisely said nothing, one of the qualities that endears him to the rugby hierarchy.

With both Hayman (twenty-seven) and Chris Jack (twenty-nine) there is clear evidence of the burn-out or staleness that results from playing so many pressure games in a year. Once tests, Super 14 and provincial matches are added up, most of the top All Blacks are looking at well over thirty matches per year.

Hayman has not discounted the prospect of returning to New Zealand rugby. 'Going to Newcastle now doesn't mean I'm totally lost to New Zealand rugby,' he said. 'I'd like to think I could come back and round out my career here.' His deal with Newcastle is for three years. At the time he made the announcement he was anxious to highlight his commitment to the All Black World Cup campaign. 'Hopefully, I'll be going to Newcastle as a member of an All Blacks team that wins the World Cup, which is my immediate goal,' he said.

The fact that a player of Hayman's values and loyalty has decided to go offshore for three years at the peak of his career highlights the major problem the NZRU now has in holding its players.

When he made his debut for the All Blacks against Samoa in 2001, Hayman became the 1000th All Black. It was an appropriate distinction, because Hayman's play is characteristic of many of the great All Blacks who have preceded him. Strong, silent, humble and totally uncompromising, he is the ultimate team man. The fact that a player of his values and loyalty has decided to go offshore for three years at the peak of his career highlights the major problem the NZRU now has in holding its players. The loss of Hayman is like losing Ken Gray or Kelvin Tremain in the 1960s, when they were at their best.

The serious and genuine attempts by the NZRU to keep Hayman in New Zealand, coupled with the loyalty and common sense that have been trade-marks of the big prop's career, illustrate how tough it will be for New Zealand to keep its top players in the future. Steve Tew virtually acknowledged this when he said the financial incentives available to All Black stars moving to UK and French teams were too good for the players to turn down. If a man with Carl Hayman's personal values chose to go, stand by for a mass exodus of others less able and less loyal.

ANDREW HORE

Why has he never quite made it?

Andrew Hore is an uncompromising hooker who came to the 2007 World Cup clearly ranked third of the three rakes within the All Black squad. Being viewed as a 'dirty-dirty' wasn't an unfamiliar role for him though, considering he'd always been in the selection frame under Graham Henry but had never been viewed as the first-pick hooker.

Hore has been a standout in recent years in a Hurricanes tight five that has struggled to provide the stable platform for which their exciting backs have been searching. He has a real knack of finding the line, as he proved in 2006 when he scored the first hat-trick by a hooker in Super rugby history. A lack of game time for the All Blacks meant that he waited 20 tests before scoring for the first time, finally achieving this during their 2007 rout of Canada.

The resurgence of Anton Oliver's career clearly affected Hore's progression within the All Blacks. This had happened previously, when Andrew was blocked from getting into the Otago team by Oliver. In 2001 Hore moved north to Taranaki and the Hurricanes. It proved a wise move, because he debuted for the All Blacks the following year against England in their 28 – 21 victory at Twickenham.

It's interesting to note that his debut remains one of only four whole matches Hore has played for the All Blacks during his career. Much like another Hurricanes hooker, Norm Hewitt, did before him, Hore is seen more on the All Black bench than he is on the field, although the substitution rules have allowed him to come off the bench much more frequently than Hewitt was ever allowed.

> **His debut remains one of only four whole matches Hore has played for the All Blacks during his career.**

Hore's most infamous moment prior to the 2007 World Cup came off the field, when he made headlines with two friends for killing a protected seal on the Otago coast — the first time anyone in New Zealand had been charged for killing a marine mammal. Hore wasn't used by the All Black selectors during the Lions series that year, and having also been out of favour in 2003, he would have breathed an extra sigh of relief when he heard his name in the 2007 World Cup squad.

DOUG HOWLETT

He's such a team man who makes the most of his ability: is there a Canterbury connection to the Auckland winger?

The player to benefit most from the conditioning programme was Doug Howlett — and he wasn't even one of the privileged. The public have always taken to their hearts any sportsman who tries his hardest when the signs are that his career is over. When he wasn't selected for the élite conditioned 22, Doug could have been forgiven for thinking he was on the way out. After all, at twenty-eight and with fifty-five tests to his name, he was probably more entitled to be conditioned than anyone. Instead of letting his omission get on top of him, Howlett used it as motivation to turn in some exceptional 2007 Super 14 performances for the Blues.

Howlett has always had a reputation for scoring tries, and started 2007 in third place on the All Blacks all-time try-scoring list. While his All Black team-mates conditioned themselves, Howlett grabbed the opportunity to secure the record for the most tries in Super rugby history. Impressive as this may be, it wasn't the element of his game that made him the 2007 darling of Eden Park.

It was his work rate and aggressive defence that stood out. On 10 March, when the Blues played against the Lions at Eden Park, Doug won over any remaining doubters. After Lions fullback Earl Rose put a cheap shot on him it appeared as though Howlett would have to be replaced, but he toughed it out. Shortly after Rose ran at Howlett, only to be smashed by a magnificent crunching tackle. Rarely has the Eden Park crowd roared its approval so loud or so long.

Howlett has always had a reputation for scoring tries, and started 2007 in third place on the All Blacks all-time try-scoring list.

Initially, speed obtained from an athletics background was the main asset that got Howlett to the top in rugby. While time has taken away some of that, his experience and courage mean the All Blacks don't lose much when he is on the field. Surprisingly for a player who's been around a long time, Doug remains a poor punter of the ball and, despite having introduced a stiff grubber and centring kick into his repertoire, kicking remains a clear weakness to his game.

Although you get fed-up with all the spin dished out by the All Black management about the number of leaders in the team, Howlett is the genuine thing. He has developed into a model professional rugby player and maximizes the use of the natural talent he has been given.

CHRIS JACK

Will he ever fulfil his potential?

Chris Jack's departure from New Zealand rugby for English club Saracens may leave a number of All Black fans asking the question 'Just how much better could he have been?' That might be churlish given his record of over sixty caps for the All Blacks, five Super rugby titles with the Crusaders and his award in 2002 of New Zealand Rugby Player of the Year.

However, the question is a reasonable one, because frequently in the past three seasons Chris Jack has looked tired, almost shattered, as he goes through the motions. Even in this mood he is better than most — but you couldn't help sense he was 'playing for tomorrow' or holding a little back.

Frequently in the past three seasons Chris Jack has looked tired, almost shattered, as he goes through the motions.

Chris is a casualty of too much football. The Crusaders' success meant that most years he played at least two more pressure matches than his main opposition. Until 2007, when he damaged his hamstring against the Waratahs in Sydney, he had been relatively injury-free, which consequently meant he started most games. Probably no one welcomed the conditioning window so much as him.

At his best he is sublime. He is strong aerially at lineout and kick-off, a good scrummager, a sure tackler and a splendid support runner. One feat of athleticism he achieved was soaring high near the sideline against the Lions to gather the ball and throw it to a support player. It could only be described as freakish.

Chris Jack probably never had the inclination nor the desire to be the next Colin Meads, but he had the physique, the skills and the speed to get to the top. To some extent his progress might have been hindered by the lack of a regular locking partner. While 'Pinetree' had his brother Stan, and Ian Jones and Robin Brooke made up the second row for the All Blacks for seasons, Jack has struggled to find a regular partner.

Jack has been the victim of his own early success. It used to be that locks didn't make the All Blacks until their mid-twenties and peak until their late twenties, early thirties. Chris was only twenty-two when he made his debut against Argentina on 23 June 2001 in Christchurch. It was a mere sixteen months later that he received the New Zealand Rugby Player of the Year award. It would be wrong to imply it has been downhill since then; but it would be equally incorrect to suggest Jack has kicked on to new heights. He hasn't, and more's the pity.

BYRON KELLEHER

Would he be more effective if he came onto the field after the haka?

Despite the fact that Byron Kelleher is one of the most capped All Black halfbacks, some real questions remain about his rugby nous, his ability to read a game, sum up a situation and — more specifically — give his team a victory in a tight situation. It could be that he gets himself so screwed up with emotion and passion that he fails to think at crucial times.

When you watch Byron quivering with emotion, his face contorted as he lustily bellows the national anthem and screams out the haka before the match, you wonder if he is going to have himself under control enough to direct his forwards and link with his backs at any time in the eighty minutes to follow.

World Cups have been won by teams with a very different type of halfback: David Kirk, Rhodes Scholar; Nick Farr-Jones, university graduate, highly articulate and a brilliant leader; Joost van der Westhuizen, with gunslinger eyes and an ice-cold logical assessment of any given rugby situation; George Gregan, who most All Black fans say is a cheat — the highest praise possible; and Matt Dawson, who remains England's most-capped scrum-half and, like Gregan, has captained his side and manipulated refs all round the world. Against this 'line-up', Byron simply doesn't cut the mustard.

If the halfback is to be the general carefully calculating the next assault, Byron isn't your man.

That is not to say that Kelleher isn't a good halfback or a good person, but if the halfback is to be the general carefully calculating the next assault, Byron isn't your man. He is more the sergeant going over the top of the trench, responding to the heat of the battle and not too worried if anyone follows him or not.

Consequently his strong, feisty play close to the ruck and maul — where he often seems more intent on being a fourth loose forward — is the overriding feature of his game. Sadly he doesn't possess the finesse of the chess master able to strategize three moves ahead.

Byron has survived in top rugby because of his natural physical attributes. He is tough, strong and nuggety, and possesses a solid kicking game. His courage in tackling means no one could ever doubt his commitment or his loyalty to the team cause. These attributes can also be his downfall. When the pressure goes on Byron suffers tunnel vision, and instead of moving the ball into space, he tries to beat the opposition on his own round the ruck. That sometimes works at provincial level, but not at test level.

Byron has survived in top rugby because of his natural physical attributes.

Kelleher is at his best when the game plan is being strictly adhered to and he is being given the space to play exactly the way the coach told him. That is when his pass is sure and clean, his runs strong and powerful and his tackles sure and hard. However, when the game plan falls over, Byron cannot change the pattern even though he's had nine years of test rugby.

SIONE LAUAKI

Is this a man or a bulldozer?

Next to Andrew Ellis, Sione Lauaki was the biggest surprise in the All Blacks 2007 World Cup squad. His chances of selection had looked dead and buried after inconsistent form and injury meant he hadn't been involved with the 2007 All Blacks in any way prior to the announcement of the final squad. Henry knew he was taking a risk. He also knew that if it paid off it would be more than worth it. On his day Sione Lauaki is like a cross between Jonah Lomu and Buck Shelford, bumping off players like a bulldozer — and he's bumped off the best.

Richie McCaw is the best of the best, but in the Super 14 match between the Chiefs and the Crusaders in 2007 McCaw was subjected to such a powerful Lauaki fend that he ended up on his backside. In this match and a prior one against the Sharks, Sione Lauaki destroyed players. After the game, Sharks coach Dick Muir commented that Lauaki had ruined his team's chances for the second year in succession. It was a big compliment coming from the coach of a South African team with such huge forwards.

On his day Sione Lauaki is like a cross between Jonah Lomu and Buck Shelford, bumping off players like a bulldozer.

Lauaki's match-winning qualities were stressed back as far as 2004 when the brilliant former All Black flanker Michael Jones, who was coaching the Pacific Island team, said Lauaki had to be included in the All Blacks. Since then injuries have limited his appearances and there are real doubts as to whether he can go eighty minutes. Such is his strength and impact, however, twenty minutes might be enough.

By selecting Lauaki, Henry limited his 'what ifs'. A loss to South Africa without Lauaki in his squad could have left him with years of sleepless nights. By taking Lauaki, he could look back with the confidence that nothing was left in the tank back at home.

BRENDON LEONARD

Proof that cream — especially from Mooloo country — eventually rises to the top?

Brendon Leonard is a Waikato man born and bred, stemming from an area of New Zealand as parochial and passionate about their rugby as it's possible to be. The Mooloo mob have been known to turn the Eden Park terraces into their own cow shed full of red, black and yellow cow bells.

They've been waiting for another home-grown hero for a while — a dinkum Waikato boy from the land of Jersey cows and thoroughbred stud farms. In Leonard they just might have found him. The heritage is there. He was born in Morrinsville, home of the famous Clarke family, and his father Ron played twenty games for Waikato in the '70s.

Hamilton and Waikato seem to be a little off the beaten track for selectors, which probably explains why he was never chosen in the national age-group teams. True Mooloo folk would argue this is par for the course, and give you a list of Waikato men headed by Duane Monkley and George Nola who should have been All Blacks. They have a point, and it serves to highlight how well Brendon played during Waikato's 2006 provincial season and the 2007 Chiefs matches. Well enough, in fact, to pass Andrew Ellis, Jimmy Cowan and Piri Weepu for the second halfback position in the squad.

Leonard quickly showed he wasn't prepared to sit back and make up the numbers. His real chance came against South Africa when he came on thirteen minutes into the second half for a poorly performing Piri Weepu. His impact was immediate, and he scored an excellent try that ensured the All Blacks finally established superiority over a virtual Springbok B team that had kept them try-less for most of the game.

Just as important as determining the future of his own career was the impact this match had on Weepu. It soon became apparent that Leonard's rise had been so fast and so convincing that the selectors no longer needed Weepu. In a World Cup campaign planned meticulously, there had been very few surprises — and no one had predicted such a rapid change of heart by the selectors.

> It soon became apparent that Leonard's rise had been so fast and so convincing that the selectors no longer needed Weepu.

One thing Leonard gave the All Blacks as they headed off to the Cup was someone largely unknown internationally. He provided an interesting challenge for opposing teams' video analysts, and gave the All Black selectors an interesting option — should they use him off the bench or should they start with him?

LUKE MCALISTER

Will he regret forfeiting his chance of greatness for a pile of paper carrying the Queen's portrait?

Luke McAlister's World Cup build-up was plagued by speculation about his future, coupled with further insecurity brought about by the All Black selectors' inability to decide where to play him. Yet he rose above all this and showed what a talented player he is, to secure the number-one second-five position ahead of Aaron Mauger going into the 2007 World Cup.

At a time when McAlister needed steadying influences all round him in 2007 he seemed to be surrounded by middle-aged rugby men who didn't have a clue how to advise him. His father Charlie, who acted as his manager, had resigned from the head coaching position with Manawatu and there was a suggestion that he was trying to negotiate a deal with a northern-hemisphere club that would have jobs for both him and Luke. Whether this was true or not, every week through the Super 14 and Tri-Nations a story would appear in print that Luke McAlister was off to clubs all over Europe. When he eventually did sign with the Sale Sharks the news didn't become official until weeks after the media had already broken the story.

If this wasn't distracting enough, the All Black selectors continued to move him around various positions, only matches out from the World Cup. Even Henry himself had acknowledged that second-five was his best position, but the desperation to find a centre led to him being tried one position further out in the backline. This was the same man who the same selectors had trialled one position further *in*, at first-five, only a few years earlier.

From the sideline it appears that paternal and selecting influences have made Luke McAlister confused, unsure and brittle.

All of this highlights the dilemma surrounding McAlister, who epitomizes the type of talent the New Zealand rugby system continues to produce. He possesses wonderful skills, great power, fabulous athleticism and plenty of pace. He's come right through the NZRU élite system, yet the people who should be giving him the structure and certainty to become a great All Black haven't been able to do that. From the sideline it appears that paternal and selecting influences have made Luke McAlister confused, unsure and brittle. The truth is that in the past, second five-eighths with a fraction of his ability have played for years for the All Blacks.

McAlister is an instinctive player who needs to be tutored in the playing and reading of a game. It is an indictment of the New Zealand system that so far he hasn't been. While New Zealand has great depth in its rugby, to lose a player of such exceptional talent at age twenty-three is something New Zealand rugby cannot afford if it wishes to remain at the top. He may return to New Zealand and chase selection for the 2011 World Cup, but in the meantime he will be sorely missed.

LEON MACDONALD

How many more lives does he have?

Leon MacDonald is an All Black survival story. His versatility and a series of injuries have meant MacDonald's All Black career has lacked the continuity of many of his Crusader team-mates. Yet it is a credit to MacDonald's ability and strength of character that he continues to bounce back from the many obstacles that have stood in his way.

His play sums up the characteristics that have made his Canterbury and Crusaders teams so successful. He is consistent, puts his team first and plays intelligent rugby. You never see MacDonald run the length of the field or beat five men to score, but he'll often beat the first tackler and set up tries for others through his selfless play.

MacDonald's performance at centre in the crucial semi-final loss to Australia at the 2003 World Cup has seen him unfairly allocated blame for the All Black loss.

While MacDonald has been used successfully as a utility in Super rugby and at NPC level, the same can't be said for his performances at test level. In particular his performance at centre in the crucial semi-final loss to Australia at the World Cup has seen him unfairly allocated blame for the All Black loss. In reality, if anyone was to blame it was John Mitchell and Robbie Deans. In more recent times Graham Henry fell into the same trap, as he unsuccessfully used MacDonald at first-five during the 2005 Tri-Nations.

> **When given the opportunity to play in his preferred fullback spot, he again showed he would be of value to the All Blacks as they planned their campaign for the 2007 World Cup.**

MacDonald may be the trendsetter for future All Blacks. After the 2003 World Cup he took up a two-year contract with Japanese club Yamaha. Niggling injuries, which included concussions, were highlighted as the main reason for him turning his back on New Zealand rugby. He returned to New Zealand just one year into his contract and commented on how refreshed he felt, both mentally and physically. His Super 12 form in his first season back indicated that his time away had done him the world of good, and when given the opportunity to play in his preferred fullback spot, he again showed he would be of value to the All Blacks as they planned their campaign for the 2007 World Cup.

Throughout 2006 Leon helped the All Black selectors with their problematic position of centre. Every time they seemed to be at their wits' end about who to play in the position, they would move in Mils Muliaina and put Leon back to fullback in the knowledge he could do nearly as well there as Mils. This was great for Leon — but it also helped to ensure the centre problem dragged on through the year.

He returned from the 2007 conditioning period a shadow of the consistent player in whom the All Black and Crusaders coaching staff had shown so much confidence. This confidence was retained through to the World Cup despite the fact he hardly played in the Tri-Nations, due to a torn groin suffered at training a few days out from the first Bledisloe test in Melbourne. The All Black selectors finally realized, when it was almost too late, that if Nick Evans had been given half the opportunities Leon had been given at fullback, they might have been able to turn Evans into an even better fullback option behind Mils Muliaina than Leon was able to provide in the crucial World Cup year.

CHRIS MASOE

Will Masoe remain a 'utility' for his entire All Black career?

Graham Henry has viewed Chris Masoe as a valuable member of his All Black squads since 2005, when he picked him for the end-of-year tour. His ability to cover anywhere in the loose forwards is the reason he's been viewed so favourably by the All Black selectors.

Considering his natural athleticism, it's somewhat surprising that he was overlooked for all national age-group and schoolboys teams. He therefore has a lot to thank for his time with the New Zealand Sevens team and franchise rugby for giving him national exposure out of Taranaki. You get the feeling that twenty years ago, before these systems were in place, he could easily have slipped through the cracks of New Zealand rugby, as has happened to many players from 'minor' provinces.

> **Considering his natural athleticism, it's somewhat surprising that he was overlooked for all national age-group and schoolboys teams.**

It was Sevens Rugby where Chris first really stood out. He played in twenty-one consecutive tournaments under Gordon Tietjens, including being a valuable member of the 2002 Commonwealth Games gold-medal-winning team, where he displayed great skill and speed for a man of his size.

Masoe's test debut came as openside flanker in the 41 – 3 thrashing of Wales in 2005. His only other appearance on that tour also came in the number 7 jersey, in the tense 23 – 19 win over England. That match ended with a nervous three minutes on the sideline for him after he became the third All Black that day to be sin-binned by Irish referee Alan Lewis.

Graham Henry's confidence in Masoe grew sufficiently in 2006 to see him used in other loose forward positions during tests. By the end of the year his form was so strong he was selected in the élite conditioning group. His return to rugby following the lay-off was disappointing, though, and he lost the momentum he'd built up in the previous two seasons.

Graham Henry's confidence in Masoe grew sufficiently in 2006 to see him used in other loose forward positions during tests.

It reached the stage where his failure to perform in both number 7 and number 8 jerseys for the All Blacks meant that it wouldn't have been a total surprise to see him omitted from the World Cup squad in favour of a specialist openside cover for Richie McCaw, like Marty Holah. This could have been even more of a prospect when the selectors decided to recall Sione Lauaki. This didn't happen, however, so Masoe took off to the World Cup with many people asking similar questions to former All Black flanker Josh Kronfeld, who said: 'Why do you want a player who can play all three back-row positions okay at international level, rather than guys who can play one of them well? Number 7 is far too important a position to carry a journeyman if the skipper is injured.'

Henry was given everything he asked for in his World Cup campaign
— there could be no excuses.

Of all the players, Justin Marshall was the most outspoken critic of Henry's rotational policy.

The Lions provided sub-standard competition and their highly anticipated campaign was a disappointment.

The clean sweep over the Lions was also a personal victory for Henry over Clive Woodward.

Graham Henry's man-management style came under the microscope, with surprising results.

Henry can sometimes come across as the headmaster dressing down a group of unruly third formers.

Finding Tana Umaga's World Cup replacement at centre dominated
Henry's campaign.

All Black legend Brian Lochore added significantly to Three Wise Men on the selection panel.

What are you on about, Graham? Are we seeing a generation gap here?

Victory in Paris against the Cockerels showed a confident team well on its way to the 2007 World Cup.

Henry had to work on his relationship with the players.

Again and again Henry was called on to defend his key campaign strategies.

Mastery of basic skills and superior fitness were key goals during the campaign.

As their campaign victories mounted under Henry, the All Blacks became used to the spoils of victory.

While the haka has a special place, would some players be better directing their emotions into their game?

Getting out there and coaching is what Henry enjoys the most.

Doug Howlett and Graham Henry developed mutual respect during their time together with the Auckland Blues.

Henry has a special ability to push Ali Williams' buttons.

The extensive management team under Henry covered most bases, with one exception — fulltime waterboy.

The loneliness of the long-distance coach — the campaign has taken an inevitable emotional toll.

Graham Henry has enjoyed a good relationship with the media — most of the time.

Most of the country loves Richie McCaw and Graham Henry is no exception.

Isaia Toeava was a real favourite of the New Zealand selectors.

Would the responsibility of captaincy ultimately prove to be to the detriment of McCaw's on-field performance?

It takes some serious silverware to get all four of these men smiling at the same time.

Going into the World Cup, there were two trophies in the cabinet — would we have to wait another four years before they were joined by the William Webb Ellis Trophy?

The unthinkable result left the All Blacks dazed and the nation stunned.

AARON MAUGER

Would he have made it if he'd come from Taranaki?

Some players get on the crest of a wave and ride it for their entire career. Aaron Mauger has enjoyed the best of rides, from the time he first played for Christchurch Boys' High School, one of New Zealand's best rugby schools. He is a product of the early talent identification scheme, having represented New Zealand at Under 16s, 19s, 21s and Secondary School level. He has played for the very best teams throughout his entire career — Canterbury, the Crusaders and the All Blacks. At the same time he has been fortunate to enjoy two of the great fly-halves playing inside him, in Andrew Mehrtens and Dan Carter.

All Black backs coach Wayne Smith is a real Mauger fan, at times defending his mediocre performances.

At the same time Aaron has contributed to the success of these teams, but it is interesting to speculate whether he would have played as many tests if he'd played his rugby in Taranaki, Waikato, Wellington, or an even smaller region. There is no question he has benefited from being in the best teams surrounded by the best players.

All Black backs coach Wayne Smith is a real Mauger fan, at times defending his mediocre performances. After a good performance by Mauger against France in 2007, Smith poured on the praise, saying it was the best the second five-eighth had played for two or three seasons. Sadly no one present from the media felt inclined to ask why Aaron had retained his place if he'd been out of form for *that* long.

The midfield area has remained the Achilles heel of Henry's All Blacks. Ever since the loss of Umaga there has been no real leader to organize and stiffen the defence and call the shots on attack.

Mauger's experience in over forty tests would suggest that he should be capable of doing this, but there is no consistent evidence to show this has happened.

To be fair to Aaron, he has been asked to play with an excessive number of players outside him and this has not allowed the development of any true combination. In modern times the best midfield combinations were Tim Horan and Jason Little for the Australians, and Frank Bunce and Walter Little for the All Blacks. Both developed through spending time together.

One thing for sure is that key rivals like South Africa and Australia have continued to view the All Blacks' midfield as its weakness.

Unquestionably the All Black management see Aaron as a key leadership figure in the backline. He was named as All Blacks captain against the Barbarians in 2004 and had previously been the National Under 21 captain. Whether they've backed the right man for the position in the first place remains questionable. One thing for sure is that key rivals like South Africa and Australia have continued to view the All Blacks' midfield as its weakness.

When Mauger announced that he had signed to go to Leicester at the end of the World Cup, Graham Henry gave him a huge rap. 'He's a world-class player and has made a significant contribution as a leader both on and off the field. His decision-making ability has been integral to the All Blacks' success.' If this statement by Henry can be taken literally, it can be strongly argued that it highlights the lack of leadership in the current All Blacks. The reference to Aaron's leadership 'off the field' is particularly surprising, given the escapade he was involved in when three All Blacks went AWOL from Wales to visit a former team-mate in London. The evidence would suggest Henry's statement is based more on wishful thinking than on solid fact.

KEVEN MEALAMU

Will the tag 'impact player' from the bench mark the end of his claim to be the best hooker in the world?

Few All Blacks suffered more from the conditioning period than Keven Mealamu. This may seem a strange claim, given that Mealamu scored three tries in his first seven games for the Blues on his return, but the reality was that both David Nucifora at the Blues and later Steve Hansen with the All Blacks chose to use him as an impact player from off the bench post-conditioning.

What a waste! By the end of 2006 few would have argued that Mealamu was the best hooker in the world. He thrived on a full workload, scoring two tries in one test against the Wallabies. His exceptional work rate, his power running close to the ground, his strong scrummaging and his low body position at ruck and maul suggested he had sewn up the number-one hooking position for the foreseeable future.

Conditioning and, more importantly, being used off the bench appeared to kill the zest and X-factor that made Mealamu unique. This is not to imply that Keven didn't play well for either the Blues or the All Blacks as an impact player, but is intended to highlight the fact that the qualities which had made him a match-winner had been dulled — the edge had been taken off the formerly dynamic hooker.

Conditioning and, more importantly, being used off the bench appeared to kill the zest and X-factor that made Mealamu unique.

Mealamu played his early rugby as a flanker and was good enough to make the New Zealand Under 16s and New Zealand Schools before 1998, when he switched to hooker. The following year he made his debut for Auckland and played every game for his province until 2003, when All Black duties intervened.

He has always been a player who thrives on a heavy workload and eighty minutes of commitment. To ignore this history and turn him into a bench player in World Cup year was nothing short of ludicrous.

A delightful, quiet, unassuming man off the field, he will always support the team.

If Mealamu has a weakness, it is his lineout throwing. The execution of successful lineouts depends on the successful combination of contributions from thrower, jumper and lifter. These combinations are not improved by one of the key components warming his backside on the bench, and nor are they fine-tuned on the practice field. The only place where lineout expertise is honed to perfection is in match conditions. Throwing is a confidence action — and the less he threw in 2007, the less confident Keven looked.

Not that Mealamu ever complained, or is ever likely to complain. A delightful, quiet, unassuming man off the field, he will always support the team. He knows how hard it is to lead modern rugby players, having tried to captain the Blues in 2006 — a job too big for the combined skills of Winston Churchill, Attila the Hun and Mother Teresa. All Black conditioning robbed him of this job as well — yet another personally disappointing aspect of the World Cup year.

MILS MULIAINA

Is he more value to the All Blacks at centre or fullback?

Mils rolls his r's like a sheep-farmer from the back of Gore, and smiles as though the hot Samoan sun is warming his spirit. He appears to epitomize where most Kiwis want their country to go — a blend of cultures, at ease and happy with the direction they are going.

To a large extent he plays his rugby the same way. At times he can show the same conservative control and constructive, accurate play as Southland's All Black centre Kevin Laidlaw did in the early 1960s, then dance off both feet with giant side-steps reminiscent of the great Samoan All Black B.G. Williams.

Mils has been a fixture of Henry's teams from day one. When Henry took over as All Black coach Mils had already made the number 15 jersey his own the previous year, when he'd played in all fourteen test matches. He had shown that he possessed not only a great all-round skill base, but also the X-factor that All Black fullbacks like Christian Cullen and Jeff Wilson had displayed in the previous decade. Like Cullen and Wilson, one of Muliaina's best attributes is the great pace he shows when counter-attacking or entering the backline.

Muliaina's talents were first displayed internationally at senior level under Gordon Tietjens, for whom he played eleven tournaments as an outstanding Sevens player. By the time he brought home a Commonwealth Games gold medal in 2002, it was clear he would become an All Black.

One of Muliaina's best attributes is the great pace he shows when counter-attacking or entering the backline.

The return of Leon MacDonald from Japan to New Zealand put genuine pressure on Muliaina for the number-one fullback position. Henry even benched Mils in favour of MacDonald for the crucial first test of the 2005 Lions series, before Mils reclaimed the number 15 jersey for the second and third tests.

In 2006 he moved south from the Blues to play for the Chiefs. The Blues missed him badly that season, as a team full of talent finished in the bottom half of the competition. Once again he became a key member of the All Blacks in 2006, playing in all but one test, where he was rested against Argentina.

Mils was reported to be one of the players to benefit most from the conditioning period.

A broken bone suffered in a practice match put an end to his 2007 Super 14 season before it had started. This was made all the more disappointing as Mils was reported to be one of the players to benefit most from the conditioning period. When he eventually returned to rugby it was back at fullback. MacDonald had shown average Super 14 form, and Henry knew he was running out of time to confirm who he saw as the best specialist centres.

Grant Fox has long been a fan of Mils as a rugby player and prefers him at centre to fullback; however, Henry recognized that Mils brought a dangerous counter-attacking quality to the All Blacks when positioned at fullback. Muliaina's versatility has always been recognized — but he is more than a utility. Entering the 2007 World Cup, he was viewed as one of the first half-a-dozen players to be picked in any All Black side.

ANTON OLIVER

Why does he think he can solve the world's problems when he can't throw a straight lineout ball?

Anton Oliver is different. Different from any hooker; indeed different from any rugby player you are ever likely to meet. Love him or hate him, and he has his share of admirers and detractors, you could never ignore him for too long. He is interesting.

Although Oliver will disagree, there will come a time when he regrets the huge bust-up he had with Laurie Mains at the

Highlanders, a series of incidents that led to a feud which sadly weakened Otago rugby. Sad, because both men had contributed so much to the game. It speaks volumes for the respect that Graham Henry has for Oliver that he was prepared to recall him to the All Blacks despite the hooker's reputation in some rugby circles of being a self-centred stirrer.

In fact, Henry has asserted on a couple of occasions that part of Oliver's role in the team is to mentor and counsel younger players. Anton has the experience to do that — he's played over fifty tests dating back to 1998, he captained the All Blacks ten times, and he's enjoyed the highs and lows of international sport. He is undoubtedly able to share with new players his personal respect for Australia, a country he has played against eleven times for only three wins.

Oliver's failure to consistently find his jumper and the criticism of him that followed has definitely affected his play round the field.

Oliver's lineout throwing has been his Achilles heel. It is mystifying that a player of his experience, intelligence and nous has struggled so much in this area. He has changed technique, modified his foot and hand positions and tried different timings, all without much success. If he had been throwing to a Matfield or an Eales for most of his career, things might have been different.

His failure to consistently find his jumper and the criticism of him that followed has definitely affected his play round the field. Although he may look tough and uncompromising, Anton Oliver is sensitive and the criticism hurt him. At one time Oliver looked as if he would seriously rival Sean Fitzpatrick as the greatest All Black hooker. He had all the physical attributes required to become one of the dominant players of his era — but it hasn't happened.

Anyone who reads his biography, released in October 2005, is left with the impression that this is unlikely to play on his mind. That mind is full of a lot of other stuff — all of which makes Oliver a much more interesting person than your average footballer, but one less focused on the mundane things needed to be the best hooker in the world. Will he regret that? Probably not.

Unlike Fitzpatrick, who knew what he wanted and would go to any lengths to get it, Oliver has embraced ideals, philosophies and people far removed from rugby circles. It is unlikely he will ever find what he is looking for, but it *is* likely his search will take him to places that most All Blacks have never heard of or are likely to be interested in.

KEITH ROBINSON

How can someone so tough be injured so often?

A real aura surrounds Keith Robinson. New Zealanders like their rugby players to be hard, tough, abrasive and uncompromising. Robinson is viewed as 'a real tough bugger' by both friend and foe. He is the sort of bloke you wouldn't want to mess with in a bar — and you could be certain Keith would be drinking in a *public* bar, not a private one.

He must be genuinely tough to have built up such a reputation in spite of endless back and knee injuries that have threatened to end his career. It is unlikely Keith will ever talk at length about the two back operations that marked his thirty months out of the game; that's not his style. Much of his rehabilitation on his back was done in his own gymnasium in Te Aroha. This is an action man, one who has overcome all sorts of frustrations to play the game that is such a significant part of his life.

> **Robinson must be genuinely tough to have built up such a reputation in spite of endless back and knee injuries that have threatened to end his career.**

Robinson seems to bring a certain presence to the All Black pack, not yet of Buck Shelford or Colin Meads proportions, but verging on the type of influence 'Cowboy' Shaw had on both his own team and the opposition. To put it more succinctly, Big Keith will bash and flatten anyone to get the ball.

Along with Jerry Collins, Robinson can be relied on to ensure no one in the opposition bullies the All Blacks. His piercing eyes, shaved head and grim demeanour are usually enough, but the word is if you don't believe that and you want to try him out, he can handle himself.

Keith is a product of the heartland of New Zealand rugby, having started his provincial career with second-division Thames Valley before joining Taranaki and later Waikato. Going into the 2007 international season he had still not played a test against Australia or South Africa, because of injuries.

Along with Jerry Collins, Robinson can be relied on to ensure no one in the opposition bullies the All Blacks.

Unlike most of his fellow All Black squad members, Robinson doesn't have a list of age-group representative teams on his curriculum vitae. Far from being a product of the élite identification groups, this is a bloke who learnt his trade slogging it out against hardened country forwards. To that extent he is a throwback to the past — the time when rural men made up the bulk of the All Black pack.

Following such a long lay-off from rugby, it was playing the game — not conditioning — that the All Black selectors viewed as best for him during the 2007 Super 14. Going into the international season, it initially appeared that Troy Flavell's more extensive skill-set would be preferred to Robinson's. Despite temporarily becoming part of the All Blacks' injury crisis at lock for part of the Tri-Nations, it soon became apparent that Robinson's more conservative willingness to do the basics would see him preferred to Flavell in the pecking order.

While his team-mates continue to leave in droves and take up lucrative contracts overseas, it would come as a huge surprise to see Robinson leave in the near future. He has worked so hard to get the silver fern on his chest that you can't see him giving it up to chase some extra money overseas. The biggest foreseeable threat to his position in the All Black squad will come with the return from injury next year of Jason Eaton and James Ryan. Yet as players like Chris Jack continue to go overseas, if Robinson can keep his own injuries at bay he should be assured of being in the All Black squad for the foreseeable future.

JOE ROKOCOKO

Did the 'rocket man' learn more from the lows of 2005 than all the highs?

If Graham Henry can press Ali Williams' buttons to perform when others can't, after the events of 2007 you'd have to conclude that Joe Rokocoko is another player Henry has a special ability to motivate. Like Williams, there was never any doubt that Joe would be selected by Henry in his 2007 All Blacks, despite hardly any current form. The rugby truism that 'there is no substitute for speed' is one of the more accurate. Joe's style of play epitomizes the value of speed, and as the All Blacks' fastest player he is a dangerous weapon when he is anywhere near top gear.

Admittedly, when Henry took over as coach in 2004 it was already Joe's second year as an All Black and he'd cemented his place in the team. He'd burst onto the international rugby scene sensationally in 2003, scoring an unprecedented ten tries in his first five test matches.

The ease with which Rokocoko stepped up to international play was aided considerably by him often having his Blues team-mates

Mils Muliaina and Doug Howlett on hand to aid him in the back three. He looked at ease around these men, and more willing to set the 'rocket man' alight with this comfortable base to work from. Henry picked him to start every match in 2004, and his strong form continued.

Joe's style of play epitomizes the value of speed, and as the All Blacks' fastest player he is a dangerous weapon when he is anywhere near top gear.

Then things changed. In 2005, a poor year for the Blues led to the 'rocket man' rarely offering a flicker of light. Henry dropped him from the All Blacks for the early part of the season and made him fight his way back through playing for the New Zealand A and Sevens teams. In hindsight you wonder whether Henry should have just picked him anyway — as he did later in 2007 when Joe had no form after Blues coach Nucifora's reluctance to play him on his return from conditioning.

Missing the Lions series was a shock for Joe Rokocoko. Everything had come easily and instinctively for him since he had first burst onto the scene. Henry showed he was prepared to drop a big star, and that might have been just the motivation Joe needed at that stage of his career. Once he started playing again, his form certainly proved one thing — Henry had a match-winner back on board, and barring injury, one who should be peaking around the time of the 2007 World Cup.

SITIVENI SIVIVATU

Is he still Joe's cousin, or is Joe now his cousin?

Warren Gatland believes Sitiveni Sivivatu sees things on the rugby field that other players can't see. Gatland has coached Sivivatu at

Waikato, and when he gives a player a rap it is worthwhile listening. His observation of Sivivatu's play helps to explain the Fijian's uncanny ability to find and create space. It doesn't happen solely because of his sensational pace, but more because of his unique ability to see where to go and when.

By the 2007 international season he was recognized by most people as the All Blacks' number-one winger.

Like the other Fijian flyers — Joeli Vidiri, Rupeni Caucaunibuca and Joe Rokocoko — who have brought so much excitement to New Zealand rugby in recent years, Sitiveni at times does the impossible, leaving spectators in breathless awe. He first registered on Graham Henry's radar in 2004 by scoring two tries against the All Blacks for the Pacific Islanders at North Harbour Stadium. A year later he was back at the same ground, touching down four times for the All Blacks against his Fijian cousins.

Sivivatu's all-round skill-set meant that Chiefs coach Ian Foster was prepared to use him at fullback for the Chiefs at times during the 2007 Super 14, as regular fullback Mils Muliaina struggled with injuries. By the 2007 international season he was recognized by most people as the All Blacks' number-one winger — no mean feat considering there were at least three other world-class wingers competing for that honour.

In March and April 2007 Sivivatu hit the headlines for all the wrong reasons, charged after an incident where he physically assaulted his wife. He was eventually discharged without conviction but received a formal warning from the NZRU, who instructed him to attend counselling. Within a month and a half the NZRU were singing a very different song — after Sivivatu refused some big offers from overseas and signed with New Zealand until the end of 2009, with deputy CEO Steve Tew saying, 'Sitiveni is a great talent and his decision demonstrates his commitment to New Zealand rugby.'

It must have been a relief to tie up Sivivatu, considering the attention great New Zealand wings of the past like Kirwan and Lomu have attracted at earlier World Cups. In the modern rugby environment, it's a blessing to know that a match-winner of Sivivatu's class will remain with the All Blacks for at least the next few years.

CONRAD SMITH

Conrad Smith played three and a half minutes of international rugby in 2007 — so how did he make the World Cup squad?

Conrad Smith was one of two contrasting centres Graham Henry chose for this year's World Cup squad. Isaia Toeava is young with raw natural talent to burn, but was still fine-tuning many aspects of his game in the international arena; Smith was the less dynamic, more conservative selection. His superior experience and rugby brain gave Henry the option of a man who'd make fewer mistakes, but would also be less likely to win a match by a touch of genius.

Smith would be the first to admit he was lucky. His form for the Hurricanes in the eight matches he played during 2007 was less than spectacular, and then a nagging hamstring injury meant he only played three and a half minutes of international rugby during the season prior to his World Cup selection.

Smith would be the first to admit he was lucky. His form for the Hurricanes in the eight matches he played during 2007 was less than spectacular.

Smith's 2006 year was also severely restricted by injury. A seriously broken leg incurred in the Hurricanes' second match of the season meant that the only internationals he played that year were the tests against France and Wales on the end-of-year tour.

But come selection time, the fact that centre still remained the problem position for the All Blacks team right through to the World Cup played in Smith's favour. The form he showed on the 2006 end-of-year tour remained fresh in the selectors' minds and was highlighted as the reason for his selection. Ironically, he may have benefited from being injured and therefore unable to show the poor form in internationals the selectors used as their reason for dropping a player like Piri Weepu.

It has been suggested in some quarters that Smith's superior education to most other All Black prospects helps to see him viewed favourably by the current selection panel. In 2003 he graduated with a Bachelor of Law with honours; professional rugby has prevented him from taking him up a job in this field.

Of course Smith is bright enough to work out that professional rugby players earn more than most lawyers these days — if he remains fit, expect him to keep playing rugby for many years to come, although with all the injuries he's been through, he's playing catch-up football every time he steps out on the park.

GREG SOMERVILLE

Is he the typical New Zealand prop?

It says something about the respect Greg Somerville has been able to build up in the teams he plays for, that the All Blacks were prepared to leave a position open in their squad to give him a chance to get over his Achilles tendon surgery in time for the 2007 World Cup. His ability to prop up both sides of the scrum, as well as his experience, make him a valuable asset to the squad.

Somerville is the type of forward many fans don't notice. His strengths are all in the areas that don't make the headlines.

His torn Achilles in the match against South Africa came at the end of a season in which he'd become only the third All Black prop to notch up fifty tests. Earlier, in 2006, he also hit his 100th game for the Crusaders, for whom he has been the backbone of their pack through a highly successful period.

Somerville is the type of forward many fans don't notice. His strengths are all in the areas that don't make the headlines. He scrums well, lifts adequately in the lineout, commits himself to ruck and maul, and supports the catcher at the kick-off. Occasionally in his career he has popped up with the ball in hand in open spaces and showed a surprising turn of speed over 10 or 20 metres. His real strength is that he knows what his job is and focuses on it, with a reputation for being a team man who consistently maintains his own high standards.

With the type of durability he has shown over the years, it was no surprise to see him return from such a crippling injury in the nick of time to get him to France. He may not have gone away as a starting prop, but having his experience and versatility back in the squad gives the All Blacks top-notch cover in a crucial area of the game.

RODNEY SO'OIALO

Does it matter that he often can't get across the advantage line?

Rodney So'oialo is no Buck Shelford. The way the dreadlocked Wellingtonian plays his rugby is poles apart from the way the great former All Black captain played his, yet So'oialo went into the 2007 World Cup as a crucial member of Graham Henry's team.

So'oialo's importance was two-fold. First, the trio he had built up with McCaw and Collins provided Henry's one real edge over his opponents. Second, it was one of the few positions where Henry didn't have good cover in the case of injury.

When Henry initially took over as All Black coach, Rodney

111

So'oialo had already played in seven tests. He'd only started in four of these, though, and his position was far from settled within the team. During his debut against Wales on the end-of-year tour in November 2002 he'd played at number 8 as the All Blacks strode to a convincing 42 – 17 victory, but throughout 2003 Jerry Collins was generally preferred ahead of him.

The key change for So'oialo came when Henry dropped Reuben Thorne. This opened up opportunities for players to claim the unsettled number 6 and number 8 jerseys. Henry initially elected to go with the combination of Xavier Rush at number 8 and Jono Gibbes at 6 for the two English tests. His familiarity with Rush meant he took the conservative option of picking him in this troublesome position, while Gibbes' aerial ability initially gave him the edge in the number 6 jersey.

Mose Tuiali'i's selection through 2004 was another one that affected So'oialo, establishing himself in the number 8 jersey throughout that year. Ironically the Canterbury number 8 made the team back then when he wasn't half the player he was in 2007, when he failed to make All Black selection. It was only during the end-of-year tour that So'oialo was able to get a start for the first time under Henry, and he initially got his break as blindside flanker. Eventually he was given the number 8 jersey, for the last test of the tour. Collins took over at number 6 and they paired up as they would do so many times in the years to come, for the Hurricanes and the All Blacks.

> Collins' role became crucial in So'oialo solidifying his position in the team, because of the way they were able to complement each other's play.

The Hurricanes factor shouldn't be underestimated in So'oialo's ability to cement a regular position in the All Blacks. Come 2005, So'oialo's form and his ability to combine well with Jerry Collins in the Hurricanes side that made the Super 14 semi-finals proved valuable come All Black selection time. He became the regular for 2005 and, with the exception of rotation, held his spot right through to the World Cup. Collins' role became crucial in So'oialo solidifying his position in the team, because of the way they were able to complement each other's play. In particular, Collins' ability to continually get the team over the advantage line has compensated for So'oialo's one noticeable weakness — his lack of bulk and ability to do the same.

What he lacks in some areas he more than makes up for in others. His work rate is outstanding, he is the fastest forward in the team over 40 metres, and at the breakdown his execution when fetching loose ball is not far behind that of McCaw. The flexibility he provides in his ability to play anywhere in the loose forwards also helps to make him one of Henry's most valuable men.

REUBEN THORNE

If he's as bad as some suggest, why have three All Black coaches risked their World Cup campaigns by selecting him?

If you ever want to get your face filled in, walk into any public bar in Christchurch and announce 'Reuben Thorne is the invisible man!' Short of suggesting that Carlos Spencer is good enough to do up Andrew Mehrtens' bootlaces, such an insult to the former captain of Canterbury, the Crusaders and the All Blacks is viewed as rugby heresy in the Garden City. Thorne is a favourite son, and the red and blacks love him. But is the man underrated by people outside of Canterbury or overrated by his coaches and team-mates?

In the rest of the country there are some who believe he does nothing in the game — hence the tag 'the invisible man'. Others argue that he does all the hard work and leaves the flashy stuff to the McCaws of this world. One thing is for sure: if a talkback host is short of calls, all he has to say is 'I thought Reuben Thorne played well', or alternatively 'Thorne didn't do much', and the lines will light up as listeners rush to criticize or defend him.

Steve Gordon, the former Waikato lock who played nineteen games for the All Blacks, continues to closely study videos of rugby games. Gordon has scrutinized Thorne, and believes that if others had the benefit of video analysis there would be almost universal approval of Thorne as a hard-working, highly skilled, productive loose forward.

Graham Henry has acknowledged that one of the key reasons Thorne got back in the All Blacks is that he brings security and stability to the team off the field.

Thorne is a battler. He is a rarity among the All Blacks, having never made an international appearance at age-group level. The real test of his character came when he was dropped as a player and as captain, when the All Blacks had been beaten in the semi-final of the 2003 World Cup. At that time the rugby fraternity in New Zealand went through what has become a four-year ritual of public blood-letting. Most of the venom was directed against coach John Mitchell, but Reuben received his fair share for a lack of leadership in the semi-final. Most other players would have been tempted to give it away, but Thorne went back to Canterbury and the Crusaders seemingly unaffected by all the attention.

Within a year he was back in the All Blacks, starting as a lock against the Barbarians. However, it wasn't until 22 July 2006 that he played his first test since that dramatic 2003 semi-final against Australia.

Graham Henry has acknowledged that one of the key reasons Thorne got back in the All Blacks is that he brings security and stability to the team off the field. Obviously his leadership record of twenty-two test matches as captain for eighteen wins is the type of experience Henry needs in his squad.

There are also a couple of statistics you should keep in mind before you make any rash statements about Reuben in Christchurch. He led the Crusaders for the inaugural Super 14 title in 2006 — to claim his sixth title and an unprecedented eight Super rugby finals appearances. The first year he captained the Crusaders in 2002, they won all thirteen matches. In 2006 he played every minute of all fifteen Crusaders games as they marched to another championship. In light of these types of statistics, unless you can personally better them, you are probably better to say nothing and just drink your beer.

NEEMIA TIALATA

With Hayman off overseas, will he finally become an AB starting prop?

Neemia Tialata is one of the biggest and strongest All Blacks to don the black jersey in many years. Going into the 2007 World Cup he was clearly ranked behind the starting props Hayman and Woodcock, but his ability to cover both sides of the scrum — coupled with his durability — made the specialist tighthead a valuable asset in the All Black squad. He currently has forty-six consecutive matches for the Hurricanes to his name, all the more significant due to the steel he brought to a Hurricanes pack that was viewed as soft before he came along.

> **Tialata's ability to cover both sides of the scrum — coupled with his durability — made the specialist tighthead a valuable asset in the All Black squad.**

With Carl Hayman's well-publicized departure overseas, Tialata became a key signing for the NZRU in June this year when they retained the Wellingtonian through until after the 2011 World

Cup. At the time he highlighted his determination to become a regular starter in the All Blacks, as well as unfinished business with Wellington and the Hurricanes, as the main reasons for making the commitment.

Now that he has served an apprenticeship under one of New Zealand's greatest tightheads, it is going to be fascinating to see whether Tialata can make the position his own and also maintain the high standards Hayman has set.

ISAIA TOEAVA

Why do the selectors call him their special project?

The All Black selection panel has consistently talked up Isaia Toeava as an extraordinarily talented player. They have put themselves on the line by continuing to persevere with him in their problem position of centre, but there is no doubt in my mind that he was initially picked too early for the All Blacks.

There is a group of fanatical All Black supporters who respond to every All Black loss with the catch-cry 'It's time they gave the young blokes a chance.' Any self-respecting analyst should in future merely reply with two words — Isaia Toeava.

> There is no doubt in my mind that Toeava was initially picked too early for the All Blacks.

The All Black selectors argue that 'Ice' is a 'special' player, and awards like the 2005 IRB Under 19 Player of the Year have recognized this. Despite that, the stark fact remains that those qualities were almost obliterated by his premature promotion to the All Blacks. In simple terms, he was not ready. His development since then hasn't been helped by having to play in a number of positions. He played second-five for New Zealand Under 19s, primarily fullback for the

Hurricanes, second-five and centre for the Blues, fullback for the All Blacks on debut and centre on other occasions. Such changes are unlikely to assist the growth of a player's confidence.

The whole episode has been a huge test of the young man and provided a steep learning curve. There were signs during the 2007 Super 14 that he had put the nightmares behind him. Undoubtedly he has great pace and strength. Hopefully he will become the 'special' player the selectors have been promising us. And if that does happen, it will be despite his selection in 2005 and 2006, not because of it.

ALI WILLIAMS

Will Ali ever learn to push his own buttons and be a team man?

If they were not from different generations, you could be forgiven for believing that Andy Haden and Ali Williams are two peas from the same pod, although it would need to be a huge pod.

Both locks have displayed tremendous athleticism, brilliant aerial skills, wonderful hands, good eye–ball coordination and the ability to do the unexpected successfully on the field. Off the field both are free spirits whose independence, personality and strength of character have seen them at loggerheads with the red tape, bureaucracy and blazers controlling rugby. Andy was before his time. Ali's time may never come.

> Ali's extrovert character and abundant abilities make him a potential match-winner, but the highs also come with lows — unpredictability, inconsistency and self-centredness that can make him a liability.

Whether Williams has the sharp street-cunning that made Haden both a wonderful survivor in and around rugby circles and a highly successful businessman, only time will tell. Meanwhile, Ali can be personable, enthusiastic, bright, lively, confident, completely over-the-top and larger-than-life. When these qualities are channelled or harnessed Williams is a wonderful, vibrant character to be around, but when they flip over the edge he is a disaster about to happen. His extrovert character and abundant abilities make him a potential match-winner, but the highs also come with lows — unpredictability, inconsistency and self-centredness that can make him a liability.

Graham Henry knows how to push all of Ali's green buttons and get him to 'go'. As Grant Fox has rightly pointed out, when Ali learns how to do that for himself he will be a great lock. When this opinion was passed on to Ali, at the height of his crisis with the Blues in 2007, he candidly responded, 'Foxy's got it right.'

It is unlikely the full story behind Ali being banished from the 2007 Blues team will ever be made public, although it is certain that if his career prospers to the extent of his potential and he becomes a great All Black, he will give his version of it in any book written about his rugby career. It will make interesting reading.

What *is* apparent is that when Ali came out of the conditioning period he was desperate to get straight back into Super 14 action. The Blues had been performing well, and coach David Nucifora argued that he couldn't justify changing a winning team. The other All Blacks similarly affected probably didn't like being on the bench either, but they kept their thoughts to themselves. Not Ali — it's not his style. No sooner had he got the first bench splinter in his backside than he was saying how desperate he was to play again.

To even the most casual observer David Nucifora and Ali Williams were on a collision course. The less game time he had, the more he alienated himself from the team, with a series of misdemeanours. The Blues' chief executive and former All Black captain, Andy Dalton, outlined that on at least four occasions the big lock had been warned but continued to act inappropriately.

When Williams arrived home from South Africa after his dismissal from the Blues squad, he was greeted by a media circus. Any parallels with the Keith Murdoch banishment of the 1970s that forced the Otago prop into hiding in the Australian outback were quickly dismissed. Ali fronted the media with Rob Nichol, the boss of the New Zealand Rugby Players' Association, at his side and his lawyer David Jones hovering in the background. The most significant thing Williams expressed at that conference was his desire to help the All Blacks win the World Cup. If Graham Henry knew how to push the right buttons on Ali Williams, he now also had him on a tight lead.

He's the type of player who loves the big stage, someone much more likely to play well in front of grandstands packed with 70,000 people than a sideline sprinkled with 70.

Ali showed how much he valued his All Black jersey by being one of the few players to give a commanding display in the first 2007 test, against France. Sadly he fractured his jaw in the following game when attempting a front-on tackle on French number 8 Sebastian Chabal. He was sorely missed throughout the Tri-Nations as the All Blacks' locking depth was put to the test.

It was always vital that he was fit for the World Cup. He's the type of player who loves the big stage, someone much more likely to play well in front of grandstands packed with 70,000 people than a sideline sprinkled with 70. This was clearly illustrated by his 2005 man-of-the-match performance in the first test against the Lions. The try he scored then signalled to both teams and all the fans that the much-vaunted Lions' tight five were in for a hiding.

Williams is the only lock in the current All Black pack who can better Victor Matfield and the Springbok lineout. If he is to do that, he'd be well advised to visit Andy Haden. Ali needs a pressure-cooker course in street-cunning and nous if he is to survive both on and off the field. There could be no better mentor than Andy.

TONY WOODCOCK

Can he retain his old-fashioned love of rugby in the modern environment?

If you're ever invited to a card game in Helensville, west of Auckland, make sure there isn't a big bloke with an innocent baby-face sitting at the table opposite you. Tony Woodcock has a poker face and gives away nothing. Few referees have been able to detect him pushing sideways after the front rows have hit. Those who have suspected Woodcock of boring-in are reluctant to penalize the man whose expression never changes and who never draws attention to himself.

Scrum coach Mike Cron declares Woodcock the 'unsung hero' of the All Black pack — athletic, intelligent, has a good physique and scrummages well. This is all backed up by a good attention to detail and a willingness to improve all the time.

At scrum time Tony is an outstanding exponent of the principal dual functions of a loosehead prop. On his team's ball he provides the bridge for his hooker and keeps the scrum stable. On the opposition's ball he works on the tighthead prop, doing everything he can to unsettle his opponents' feet and legs.

> **At scrum time Tony is an outstanding exponent of the principal dual functions of a loosehead prop.**

It has been commonly believed that props don't mature until their late twenties, and few make it into top rugby until they are in their mid twenties. Not Woodcock. He first propped the Blues scrum at the age of just twenty and made his All Black debut while still twenty-one, following a successful development through New Zealand age-group teams. It was missing New Zealand secondary school selection that first got him serious about his rugby, and the memory of that disappointment has remained a motivational factor for him ever since. 'It's disappointing when you miss out on a national side you'd really wanted to make,' he has said. 'You can't afford to be left out because it's a hard road back, so you have to make sure while you're here, you work as if you *have* missed out.'

This philosophy goes a long way to explaining his consistently high standard of play. It also explains his commitment to the North Harbour jersey — an attitude not always shown by other high-profile Harbour players in recent years. Tony played every minute of every North Harbour game between 2001 and 2004, with the exception of the first two matches of 2004 when he was required for All Black duty.

In 2006 he endeared himself to Harbour fans for all time by requesting permission to return early from his enforced rest due to All Black duty to play in North Harbour's Ranfurly Shield challenge. His role in securing that victory and bringing the shield to North Harbour cannot be overestimated.

Tony Woodcock is already a world-class prop, and with his attitude, commitment and durability he may go on to become one of the best New Zealand has produced.

The Helpers

One of Graham Henry's best skills is his ability to identify and select good people to work with him. As All Black coach he had never had it easier — the best want to work with the All Blacks, and he had his pick.

- Do you really need a sixteen-man management team for just thirty players?

- What do all the management team *do*?

- Will Henry's successor come from within this group?

A KEY POINT when assessing the management's personnel and structure is to acknowledge that no All Black coach has ever been given so much by the NZRU. Graham Henry should be very grateful for the fact that the CEO during his time as coach has been Chris Moller — a man whose own personal goal has been the winning of the Rugby World Cup on his watch. It is not too far from the truth to say that everything Henry has asked for, Henry has got.

Coach — Graham Henry
Assistant coach — Wayne Smith
Assistant coach — Steve Hansen
Selector — Sir Brian Lochore
Specialist skills coach — Mick Byrne
Specialist scrum coach — Mike Cron
Technical analyst — Andrew Sullivan
Head strength and conditioning coach — Graham Lowe
Strength and conditioning coach — Ashley Jones
Team manager — Darren Shand
Baggage manager — Errol Collins
Media manager — Scott Compton
Doctor — Deborah Robinson
Muscle therapist — George Duncan
Physiotherapist — Peter Gallagher
Sports psychologist — Gilbert Enoka

There are sixteen people named in the All Blacks management group in the 2007 All Blacks Media Guide. When they hear this, former All Blacks shake their heads in a mixture of disbelief, frustration and even anger. The 'oldies' believe it is a squandering of money that could be better used in developing the game. Some argue that with so many voices a clear, strong message won't get through. Others are quick to point out that if you're paying someone a salary and giving them a title, they feel they must be doing something even if there is nothing there to do.

The most obvious criticism is that with so many involved in management it is unlikely that genuine leadership will develop in the team. Is Richie McCaw's a more powerful voice in the team than the individual voices of Steve Hansen, Wayne Smith, Sir Brian Lochore, Mick Byrne and Mike Cron? Are the players confused by advice and information from too many people?

The most obvious criticism is that with so many involved in management it is unlikely that genuine leadership will develop in the team.

The hierarchy of the NZRU and the management of the All Blacks would counter these arguments by pointing out that the management groups of Australia, South Africa, France and England are just as big — and in England's case considerably bigger. But this fails to take into account the types of people involved.

There is a marvellous story about the English team going into extra time in the final of the 2003 World Cup. The captain, Martin Johnson, had the entire team around him and was laying out the strategy which would win England the William Webb Ellis trophy. Suddenly Clive Woodward arrived, and was about to interrupt when his great captain told him, 'Fuck off, Clive. We've got it all under control.' To Woodward's credit he did — and England won. In rugby, as in the heat of battle, there can be only one commander.

The short answer to all the questions and comments raised about the size of the management group is that if it has to be that big to ensure victory, and that big to support the team, then it is justified. Nevertheless, the management group is undeniably so large that managing the managers must be a task in itself.

The strongest voices in most successful teams are those of the coach and the captain. In the history of New Zealand rugby a prime example of this is the combination of coach Neil McPhail and captain Wilson Whineray in the 1960s. Wilson was hugely respected, and his words were the only ones that mattered on the field.

Graham Henry was at his most successful when he was distant from his players. There is no doubt that an evaluation report done on him in 2004 has had a profound effect. During the evaluation process, Graham was asked what his strengths and weaknesses were. To his amazement, when the players were asked the same question about him their responses were almost the direct opposite. It would be difficult to overestimate the impact this news had on him. He changed. He tried to get closer to the players, and began to delegate more. He was never quite the same coach again — never as independent, and never again prepared to act unilaterally.

At the same time, Richie McCaw is a young and inexperienced captain finding his way. A lot has been written and said about whether an openside flanker is the right person to captain a team in the modern game. It would be more meaningful to question how much of a hindrance a leadership group of eleven players and a management team of sixteen is to a young captain wanting to establish himself in the role.

Consequently, with both Henry and McCaw constrained, some key members of the management team assumed powerful roles. While Graham Lowe's contribution is covered in the chapter on the conditioning period, here is my assessment of how things work otherwise within this group.

Wayne Smith, assistant coach

Wayne Smith is intense, analytical, thoughtful, painstaking and diligent — all good qualities for an assistant coach, a role for which he is well suited. During his time as All Blacks coach Wayne's sincerity and honesty led to him publicly expressing doubts about his ability to take the All Blacks to victory in the 2003 World Cup. These doubts ultimately led to his replacement by John Mitchell. Most other coaches would never have admitted to self-doubt, hiding instead behind lies and half-truths. Sadly, Smith's scepticism was seen as weakness in many circles when it should have been interpreted as strength.

Most other coaches would never have admitted to self-doubt, hiding instead behind lies and half-truths.

All selectors and coaches have their favourites, and Wayne Smith is no exception. Top of his list are Aaron Mauger and Isaia Toeava. It is the Smith style to be loyal to the point of wearing blinkers, which helps explain why Aaron retained his place when he was out of form for so long, and why Smith persisted with Isaia. However, the inability to develop a good midfield combination must be annoying and frustrating to a backs coach who spends countless hours poring over videos.

On the other hand, Smith has been staunch in supporting the flat backline, and it has been good to hear him speak out strongly in response to the media questioning its worth.

Steve Hansen, assistant coach

Steve Hansen and Wayne Smith are like chalk and cheese. Hansen has no trouble fronting up to the indefensible, combining a mix of bluster, bravado and baloney. There was a stage when the worst areas of All Black play were lineouts and taking kick-offs, two of his specific responsibilities. To hear Steve explaining it away, one could only reach the conclusion that if he ever got the boot from rugby coaching, he would certainly make it in politics.

Not that this is likely. This is the heir-apparent to the coaching throne, a man who enjoys a very close relationship with the deputy

CEO of the NZRU, Steve Tew. A number of insiders believe that, come the time to replace Henry, Hansen will be appointed without the job being advertised. There is a recent precedent for this in Steve Tew's own appointment to CEO designate.

Steve Hansen's inability to get the All Black lineout functioning properly necessitated former AB lock Robin Brooke being called in to assist. As covered later in this book the results were almost immediate, suggesting strongly that Hansen had been out of his depth. At that time his international test coaching record with Wales of thirty-one tests for just eleven wins — and thus twenty losses — came into focus.

Steve Hansen's inability to get the All Black lineout functioning properly necessitated former AB lock Robin Brooke being called in to assist.

Hansen is extremely popular with the players, and in the rugby environment he thrives on the camaraderie, the fellowship and the banter that is so much a part of it. Going into the 2007 World Cup, however, his areas of responsibility remained a major weakness in the All Black game.

Sir Brian Lochore, selector

Sir Brian Lochore is the fourth selector on the All Black panel, along with Henry, Smith and Hansen. Although Sir Brian had been out of coaching for over a decade, his appointment was one of the shrewdest moves Graham Henry has made. Having an iconic figure assisting with selections dissuaded many journalists from criticizing the selectors.

Lochore has had a direct impact on the members of the squad, mentoring some of them and ensuring they are aware of the traditions and history of the All Blacks. He has spent a lot of time working with Gilbert Enoka, the All Black sports psychologist. 'He's the trained psychologist and I suppose I'm the bush psychologist,' Lochore explains. 'We talk to the players about anything they want to talk about or we want to talk about with them.'

Gilbert Enoka, sports psychologist

Enoka has been with the All Blacks since 2000, in the most mis-understood role in the entire management group. The average rugby fan cannot understand why the All Blacks need a 'shrink'. Derogatory comments about couches and making them soft, and the totally done-to-death 'Colin Meads would have told them where to put their couch' and 'What would a shrink who plays volleyball know about footie?' overwhelm talkback the moment Gilbert Enoka's name is raised. Such comments are totally unwarranted and unjustified. In all discussions with former Black Cap cricketers and current All Blacks about Enoka, there is nothing but praise for his style, values and results.

He sees his role with the team as a dual one of mental skills coach and the development of team support. On the one hand he has set up a system of routines to enable each player to perform at his highest individual level, while on the other he is responsible for developing leadership within the group. These areas interrelate and he manages their mix superbly.

> In all discussions with former Black Cap cricketers and current All Blacks about Enoka, there is nothing but praise for his style, values and results.

Enoka stresses that the All Black squad faced a crisis at the end of the Tri-Nations in 2004. 'The team and management realized after the two comprehensive defeats that we needed to radically change,' he explained. New and extensive efforts were made to help the players become open and honest. Enoka went to some lengths to explain the process of mental development the All Black squad had gone through:

'In September 2004 we began to try to break down the macho image. We then moved into the growth stage of identifying needs at both individual and team levels. This was the start of our project to get the group ready for France, and aimed at making sure the players were equipped for the World Cup as people, and that they had the tools to succeed as sportsmen. The day the World Cup squad was announced we moved out of the growth and into the achievement stage. This achievement stage is accepting where you are at and making your goal the delivery of the World Cup.'

The All Blacks have addressed the 'choker' tag during the last three years. Enoka thinks the management team has encouraged the players to recognize that there is more to life than just rugby. They developed the mantra 'Rugby is what we do, not what we are.' It was thought that if the players could be comfortable with where they were at, they would be better able to put the challenge of France into perspective. At the same time, the management team felt it was vital that the team knew how passionate Kiwis were about the quest for the World Cup.

The All Blacks have addressed the 'choker' tag during the last three years.

Enoka is forthright about the change in attitude of the All Blacks. 'Before the watershed of 2004 the All Blacks thought of themselves as part of the stereotype rugby player [image] of booze, birds and parties. That changed after September 2004, and the All Blacks began to act differently, both individually and as a team,' he asserted. For the eighteen months before the 2007 World Cup started, the All Blacks were put through a set of tests or experiments to test their decision making under pressure. The leadership group was taught that it always had an option to turn to, with the theme throughout that a performance culture is all about accountability.

At the same time, Enoka is prepared to acknowledge that there have been glitches along the way, with the biggest of these perhaps the most important development lesson of them all. 'The defeat at Melbourne [in June 2007] showed us that we were not bullet-proof, and it made us look at our leaders,' he explained. Enoka believes that the entire group had placed too high an emphasis on winning in South Africa and subsequently were not prepared for the Wallabies.

Enoka admires Henry. 'One important thing I have learnt from this campaign is that the gap between a fifty-year-old and a sixty-year-old is unbelievable. It is amazing the amount of wisdom that comes with age,' he explained. Enoka acknowledged the critical changes Graham Henry made to his style of coaching after the September 2004 evaluation, but for professional reasons would not be drawn on what precipitated those changes. However, he was prepared to concede that the All Blacks now operate on a shared leadership basis and that 'Ted's [Henry's] ego doesn't necessitate him being at the top of the tree.'

Up until three years ago, Enoka believes the All Blacks had too much done for them and had become dependent on others to do everything — including making their decisions. He thinks this has now stopped, with Richie McCaw and the leaders taking responsibility for what happens on the field.

Enoka is the exact opposite to what most sports fans think a sports psychologist would be like. He is not an idealist, nor a theorist talking in jargon or riddles. Gilbert Enoka is a positive pragmatist doing his best to prepare a group of athletes for their ultimate challenge.

Mick Byrne, specialist skills coach

Mick Byrne wouldn't have got a job with the All Blacks twenty years ago for two reasons. First, he has no background in rugby union, having played Aussie Rules for Melbourne, Hawthorne and Sydney for fifteen years. Second, any self-respecting coach in the amateur era would have vigorously asserted that any player who couldn't kick or catch would never make it into the All Blacks.

Byrne is employed with the NZRU as a 'specialist skills coach'. He was the Wallabies' catching and kicking coach when they won the Rugby World Cup in 1999, and he did the same job from 1998 to 2001 with the Brumbies. He worked with the Springboks, Scotland and the English club Saracens before joining the NZRU high-performance team in 2005, where his job description specifies that he works on the overall skills of all the players in the New Zealand franchises in the specialist area of kicking and catching.

Since January 2006 Byrne has been working hard with New Zealand players to bring the spiral punt back into the game.

Byrne is quick to point out that with the increased emphasis on defence in rugby over the past five years has come the obligation to stop the opposing team kicking. As a result, most international sides now have specialist coaches teaching players the art of kicking from the hand.

Since January 2006 Byrne has been working hard with New Zealand players to bring the spiral punt back into the game. He sees it as not only a tremendously long kick, but also a good kick into the corners for players to run onto. Byrne thinks the drop-punt has become more prevalent over the last few years because the pressure has been on an accurate kicking game.

Mick Byrne also believes that kicking is used more today to break down defensive screens. 'In the last few years we've seen the cross-field kick, the grubber, the chip-kick and other attacking kicks used by teams to score tries and attack.' He explains that the cross-kick has become more prevalent as the game has evolved, with players like Dan Carter able to kick the ball very flat to the other side of the field. Byrne thinks that the flat backline necessitates the use of such kicks as a method of breaking down the defence.

'I spend a fair bit of time analysing the opposition's kicking abilities. I look at not only the team but the individuals' kicking traits. It helps our players to read the opposition,' he added.

When it comes to goal-kicking Byrne has firm ideas: 'I think goalkickers can be made, but if they are born they have a better chance of being good at it. It is more difficult if you don't have a natural kick, although you can help kickers to get the ball going straight and how to find their own way of finding power through the strike.'

Byrne has firm ideas: 'I think goalkickers can be made, but if they are born they have a better chance of being good at it.'

Byrne is quick to point out that Dan Carter combines all the techniques with great awareness and feel. Carter generates a lot of speed in his down-swing to give the ball more power. Consequently, he stays more compact over the ball. Byrne says that Carter is the most self-aware player he has worked with, which in practical terms means coaching tips only have to be given to him once.

Mick Byrne reinforces what many rugby fans have believed for years — goal-kicking at test level is predominantly a mental exercise.

'I would say once it comes to the match time, it's probably as much as eighty to ninety per cent. I think once you've done the technical work during the week and you get out in the game, it's about the ability to go into your kicker's mode. It doesn't matter how you're playing as a player, or the result of the game. It's one of the few closed skills performed on the rugby field. You just need to go through what you need to do and the outcome will take care of itself.'

Mike Cron, specialist scrum coach

Mike Cron, the All Blacks' specialist scrum coach, has been one of the real successes of the management team Henry has built around him. Cron first worked with the All Blacks in 2002, and in 2003 joined Steve Hansen and the Welsh team for their Rugby World Cup campaign.

Cron has developed the All Black scrum into the best in the world. It now sets the benchmark for technique, effectiveness and power-ratios. He is a stickler for good technique and set-up, and when you watch Cron take an All Black scrum practice you have to be impressed by how rare it is to see a scrum collapse. Perhaps this is because if one does go down, Cron makes every forward drag himself along the ground using only his elbows.

> **Cron has developed the All Black scrum into the best in the world. It now sets the benchmark for technique, effectiveness and power-ratios.**

Cron believes it takes four years to develop a prop, and that this development needs to be focused at specialized coaching classes with a full complement of strength and conditioning coaches. He stresses that front-rowers need to know how to react to any scrum-time situation, and that with proper coaching and repetition he believes these reactions will begin to occur naturally and instinctively.

Mike Cron is refreshingly honest about some of the recent IRB and commercial innovations affecting the scrum. He believes that the 'crouch-touch-pause-engage' has led to too many collapsed scrums because the two packs are down a lot longer in the 'set-up' position waiting for the engagement. He is equally as critical of the new skin-tight jerseys, explaining how difficult they make it for forwards to grip onto, a crucial factor in setting a good, tight scrum.

Darren Shand, team manager

It is no surprise that eight of the sixteen people responsible for managing and coaching the All Blacks have worked in the Crusader franchise — which has been by far the most successful in Super rugby history. In American professional sport, it has long been accepted that you cannot have a successful team unless the front desk is in order. The governance and management of the Crusaders has played a major part in establishing the winning culture at AMI Stadium (formerly Jade Stadium), where the emphasis has been on doing the simple things well and sticking to winning patterns. It was from this background that, in 2004, Darren Shand became All Black manager. Manager of the Canterbury NPC team from 1999, Shand was in charge of the Crusaders for four years, during which time they made every Super 12 final and won the competition twice.

Shand was never given the same power as Martin had enjoyed, nor has he the same force of personality and presence.

Shand took over the management at a time when the guidelines within which he was to operate were blurred. The NZRU had given manager Andrew Martin authority and status over coach John Mitchell, in an attempt to organize the structure on more business-like lines. However, when Martin and Mitchell fell out it meant the Union had effectively chopped the manager off at his knees. Martin resigned, to be replaced by Tony Thorpe who clearly was answerable to Mitchell.

Shand was never given the same power as Martin had enjoyed, nor has he the same force of personality and presence. His tenure has been marked by careful, meticulous planning from a low-profile position; to an observer, he appears to have a good working relationship with all his staff and, most importantly, with coach Henry. Clearly, though, it is Henry who calls the shots — the experiment during Andrew Martin's time of making the manager CEO of the All Blacks has been discarded.

Scott Compton, media manager

The man with the worst job in the All Blacks is Scott Compton, the media manager. Why anyone in their right mind would want the stress, anxiety, pain, abuse and confusion of this ultimate 'no-win' position defies explanation. No matter what he does, he will upset someone. Since the early 1990s a series of people have started this job with the best of intentions and ended their term closely resembling physical and emotional wrecks. In my opinion, I think it's highly unlikely Scott Compton will break that mould.

No matter what he does, he will upset someone.

There are a number of reasons for this. At the top of the list is the entrenched arrogance that, sadly, pervades many of the elements now surrounding the All Blacks. It is arrogance bred out of ignorance, and fostered by the dependence the media in rugby-mad New Zealand have on stories about the All Blacks. It does not exist in Australia, where the Wallabies know they must help promote their sport against the more powerful codes of league, AFL and soccer.

In New Zealand the rugby media is a crazy mix of knowledge-able writers, slimy sycophants, opportunists who wouldn't know a halfback from a fullback, writers for women's magazines, television reporters, radio broadcasters and a host of other hangers-on who wouldn't be able to describe their own jobs. All have requests, and all go to Scott Compton. Add to that the pernicious fallacy that every journalist believes their story is the most important and the most urgent, and you begin to appreciate the dilemma. The result is that no matter who fills the media liaison officer's job, they quickly become the media prevention officer in the eyes of the journalists with whom they have to work. This inevitably leads to unnecessary friction between the All Blacks and the media, with the end result that the team is often portrayed in a negative light.

> **There appears to be little, if any, effective media training done with the team. Their answers are colourless, sanitized and boring.**

Another problem Compton seems to have inherited is that many of the All Blacks are monosyllabic, with little or no idea of how to speak in public. Some appear to be limited to phrases such as 'I'm real proud of the boys' when they win, or the clichéd 'We're gutted' when they lose. There appears to be little, if any, effective media training done with the team. Their answers are colourless, sanitized and boring, with the only clear instruction I can perceive the players receiving is not to trust the media. All of which is sad. Most of the New Zealand media is as desperate as the rest of the country to see the team win, but because of both the ridiculous restrictions on interviewing players and the trite, boring answers trotted out when there *are* interviews, most journalists become very cynical very quickly about the All Blacks. That also is sad. It doesn't need to be like this, and it certainly wasn't in the days before media liaison officers.

The problem is that Scott Compton and his predecessors have all been paid by the NZRU and 'he who pays the piper calls the tune'. For a liaison officer to work effectively, half of their salary should be paid by the combined media associations, who would then have the right to have at least half the say in how and when the All Blacks were interviewed. It won't happen, for two reasons: it suits the NZRU to control the situation, and most New Zealand media organizations are so stingy they would never see the value of such a mutually beneficial arrangement.

George Duncan, muscle therapist

One of Graham Henry's biggest attributes is his ability to identify talent where others cannot. George Duncan is a perfect example. Henry heard about the magic hands of this muscle therapist and hauled George in to help out with both Auckland and the Blues. Any other coach probably wouldn't have seen the worth of the unassuming, somewhat diffident Duncan. Jerry Collins probably summed it up better than anyone else when he said, 'George Duncan is a good man. I enjoy talking to him.'

Muscle therapists are a bit like hairdressers — everyone tells them their secrets.

George has some Tongan heritage and knows intuitively what the Island boys are thinking. In turn they have confidence in him. Muscle therapists are a bit like hairdressers — everyone tells them their secrets. There is no question that some of the most important messages for the coach, particularly from the Polynesian members of the team, arrive via the muscle therapy table.

The Southern contingent

Henry and Shand are believers in acquiring people from a winning environment. From the Crusaders set-up they have acquired doctor Deborah Robinson, technical analyst Andrew Sullivan, baggage man Errol Collins, and strength and conditioning coach Ashley Jones. Completing the fulltime management team is physiotherapist Peter Gallagher, who worked with the Highlanders before joining the All Blacks.

The Cost

When people become obsessed, they lose balance. So much emotional energy is focused onto their obsession that everything else takes a back seat. Following the 2003 World Cup disappointment, New Zealand's desperation for an All Black win in France in 2007 hit obsessive levels. A 'win at all costs' philosophy prevailed, putting at risk the basic philosophies and structures that had made New Zealand such a dominant rugby nation.

- What sacrifices were made to feed New Zealand's World Cup obsession?

- How did those sacrifices affect New Zealand rugby?

- Did those sacrifices improve the All Blacks' chances of winning the World Cup?

As NEW ZEALAND headed off to France for the 2007 World Cup, most New Zealand fans asked themselves if they believed the All Blacks would win the Cup. They also asked whether one tournament lasting six weeks was worth the significant cost New Zealand rugby had incurred in the preceding four years. This was an appropriate time to ask — after the Cup, the emotional response to the result would undoubtedly influence their judgement. It always does.

Put simply, a win at the World Cup would see short-term widespread support for the campaign Graham Henry had put together, whereas a loss would see him and his players afraid to return to New Zealand. The short-term fallout would be horrendous, with no William Webb Ellis trophy to balance the massive cost to New Zealand rugby that had taken place during the previous four years. Was the cost — and I'm talking here about the whole cost, not just in monetary terms — truly worth it?

Admittedly, world rugby's growing obsession with the World Cup must also take some of the blame. However, New Zealand has led the way, often showing disregard for the effects on rugby of its short-term actions in chasing the Cup. The impact on both the Rebel Super 14 and the ANZ Cup would be difficult to overestimate — both have been adversely affected.

Many Kiwis have argued that because New Zealand rugby is so strong, it has been justified in resting and rotating players from squads and competitions in recent years. After all, it has continued to produce good results — an unusual level of arrogance that is sadly prevalent in rugby circles in this country. No matter how much the country sacrificed, there was never any guarantee this would translate into a win at the 2007 Cup — so it is perfectly reasonable to ask where it will stop. Will the obsession now be even greater to win the 2011 Cup at home? If that is the case, there will be a negative, and inevitable, impact on the grass roots of the game.

A key point many New Zealanders overlooked in the lead-up to the 2007 World Cup is just how deprived they had been of watching quality performances by their national team. In Graham Henry's defence, trying to keep his side's performances at their 2004 level right through to 2007 would have been tough. If he'd tried to do so and failed, he'd have been accused of having his team peak too early. During the 2007 Tri-Nations, former Wallaby coach Bob Dwyer observed what had happened to the All Blacks during this period:

'I thought their peak was when they destroyed France in Paris a few years ago [27 November 2004, when they thrashed the French 45 – 6 at Stade de France]. I've never seen any team play like they did for the full eighty minutes that day. So in some ways, it's inevitable they're in decline. When you are at an absolute peak, the only way you can go is down. The best they can hope to do is even out their performances so that the troughs are never too deep.'

If it weren't for the World Cup obsession, the All Blacks could have continued to search for the perfect game in the same way as the great Auckland sides of the mid-1980s.

The disappointment from a fan's perspective is that if it weren't for the World Cup obsession, the All Blacks could have continued to search for the perfect game in the same way as the great Auckland sides of the mid-1980s — they certainly had the men to do it. McCaw and Carter are two of the greatest players New Zealand has produced, and happen to play in the two most critical positions in the modern game. There is no shortage of great players around them, from Mils Muliaina at the back to Carl Hayman up front. With this sort of talent at Henry's disposal you have to believe that in 2007 especially, the All Black fan has been denied the privilege of watching a golden year of All Black rugby.

It should also not be overlooked that these substandard performances have come about at a time when world rugby has been weaker than it has been for a long time. While Henry argued that something different had to be done to win the Cup, something other All Black teams had failed to do, there is also a strong belief in some quarters that he didn't have to do anything special. The superior talent he had at his disposal would do the trick for him if he coached and selected the All Blacks in the conventional way — a way that definitely wouldn't have included rotation of players and conditioning periods.

The sacrifice New Zealand rugby has made makes even less sense when you ask yourself what the World Cup is really all about. It actually involves few meaningful matches for a side like the All Blacks. If you're lucky, you might have three matches that deserve to be called tests, but most pool matches continue to be one-way-traffic. At the same time, so much value has been placed on World Cups that test matches leading up to the Cup are now treated as warm-up matches for the Cup, rather than as true 'tests'. Just as confusing has been the way top players have been rested from matches in tournaments that are far more competitive than the World Cup, tournaments that have provided critical revenue streams for rugby since the game turned professional.

The sacrifice New Zealand rugby has made makes even less sense when you ask yourself what the World Cup is really all about. It actually involves few meaningful matches for a side like the All Blacks.

These are not so much criticisms of Graham Henry as they are of the system he has been forced to work within. He will be judged more as a coach on the results of a handful of matches at one tournament than on the four years leading up to that tournament — such is the extent of the obsession.

No one has been more outspoken about the cost to world rugby of the World Cup structure than All Black legend Sean Fitzpatrick. In a column for the *Herald on Sunday* during 2007 he wrote:

> The unrelenting focus on the World Cup — to the exclusion of other meaningful test rugby — and the growth of the power of the northern-hemisphere clubs makes me think that there is only one end for the international game. It will become like soccer. Club rugby will be where the power and credibility is. The international game will be insignificant — except for once every four years at the World Cup. Why would Little Johnny want to play rugby if he was watching the current internationals, with weakened sides, rotation, and emphasis on one set of games that occur every four years? I find myself thinking I'd rather watch Chelsea or Manchester United.

The cheapening of the All Black jersey has been another sacrifice made in the quest for the Cup. The aura associated with the All Black jersey has suffered, to the extent that the naming of All Black teams is no longer an event players or fans in New Zealand await with bated breath.

Justin Marshall was the most outspoken All Black when Henry began his extensive rotation of players. Even after moving offshore to play in the United Kingdom, he continued to criticize the system and emphasized that many other All Blacks held similar views, but elected not to express them publicly for fear of affecting their chances of selection. Aaron Mauger was one player to speak out about his frustration with rotation during the middle of the 2007 Tri-Nations. 'Yes, it is. It is frustrating, I would love to play every game, you know? It's always hard when you play one week and don't play the next week. It's hard to know if you're the man for the job, or if the coaches want something else. It's confusing more than anything at times.'

Mauger's statement was a useful insight into how many other players were feeling about rotation. Conspiracy theorists suggested his comments might have had something to do with his not being selected in Henry's 'best team' for the final Tri-Nations match, considering the praise that had been heaped on him by Wayne Smith only weeks earlier.

Jerry Collins had always spoken about his love of playing rugby and the frustration of the conditioning period, so it was less of a surprise to hear him express similar frustration during the 2007 Tri-Nations. 'You'd be bullshitting yourself if you said you weren't [frustrated], but sometimes it's just the nature of the game,' he said.

The All Black jersey retained much of its value through the early years of professionalism, but the introduction of the substitution rule played a significant role in cheapening test caps. While Graham Henry can point to a player like Brendon Leonard as someone who has thrived on the extra opportunities the rotation system has provided, an opposing argument is that neither Byron Kelleher nor Piri Weepu were given the opportunity to settle in the halfback position. Weepu especially can be seen as suffering as a result of rotation.

While rotation might keep some fringe All Blacks in New Zealand rugby, it could have also played a role in some of our top players signing overseas contracts. If they still felt they 'owned' the jersey, as Buck Shelford owned the number 8 and Sean Fitzpatrick owned the number 2, people like Carl Hayman and Chris Jack might have been more inclined to remain in New Zealand to play out their careers.

Another significant cost has been the general New Zealand public's declining interest in rugby, a direct result in my mind of the second-rate product they've been asked to watch in the period through to the Cup. This has involved not only under-strength All Black teams, but also opposition teams so weakened they had a cheek to be wearing their national jersey. The current rules of rugby are also responsible for wavering interest, but not being able to see the best players on show has been just as much of a factor in people not attending matches or tuning in on television.

Another way New Zealanders have been denied the best rugby could offer has been the NZRU's continued insistence on players playing domestically if they want to remain eligible for the All Blacks. This has denied people the chance to watch players like Bruce Reihana and Regan King at their peak. Even more importantly, players like Kevin Senio and David Hill have graced the black jersey while legends like Andrew Mehrtens and Justin Marshall were overlooked for selection because of this rule. This is hypocritical of the NZRU. If everything was really being thrown at the World Cup as they have promised it would be, then surely overseas players should have at least been available for All Black selection during the lead-up to the Cup.

The current rules of rugby are also responsible for wavering public interest, but not being able to see the best players on show has been just as much of a factor.

No one will ever be able to quantify the true benefits or costs of rotation and conditioning on Henry's All Blacks. There is a strong belief, however, that both of these systems have been responsible for keeping South Africa in the chase for the World Cup, when the door could effectively have been closed in 2006, well before the Rustenburg test.

Days before his Crusaders team played their unsuccessful Super 14 semi-final, coach Robbie Deans talked about the struggle he'd experienced within his squad when his All Blacks returned from conditioning. 'To get thrown into the middle of a competition with no pre-season background is very, very hard. And it showed through breakage [injuries] and we anticipated that. Our players spoke of the soreness they experienced. It wasn't easy but they did very well. They produced some outcomes while grappling with fitting into the mix and coping with the stresses and strains.'

'To get thrown into the middle of a competition with no pre-season background is very, very hard.' — Crusaders coach Robbie Deans

---

Deans had clearly never been a fan of what took place, but had gone along with it because realistically he had no choice. 'We supported it because that was meant to be the best thing, and we want them [the All Blacks] to succeed. But I'll give you this much, I'd like to think we won't be going through that again,' he said.

For Deans to say he hopes they don't go through it again speaks volumes. If he thought the possible benefits justified the cost he endured, he could have lived with it. That wasn't the case.

Financially the cost to New Zealand rugby in the short term has been minimal. Employing twenty-two more players during the Super 14 was a significant investment, but not massive in the scheme of a World Cup campaign. What would have *really* hurt the NZRU would have been if it had been forced to pay compensation to the broadcasters for their role in devaluing the Super 14 competition. Amazingly, they never had to pay a cent.

While the NZRU got off scot-free in the short term, the long-term financial cost could be a different story. When the NZRU — and fellow SANZA nations — come to renegotiate their next television deal, after the experiences of 2007 any sensible broadcaster will be wary of the value of the product they purchase. The long-term cost could therefore stretch into the millions.

Most of this cost is New Zealand's fault. Indirectly it can be viewed as responsible for the devaluation of the Tri-Nations as well as the Super 14. It is very unlikely that the Springboks' Jake White would have made a mockery of the 2007 Tri-Nations by resting twenty players if it hadn't been for New Zealand first leading the way by resting twenty-two of its own through half of the Super 14.

Financially the cost to New Zealand rugby in the short term has been minimal. The long-term cost could stretch into the millions.

Domestically the NZRU has also had to deal with the financial ramifications of releasing players for the conditioning programme and the World Cup. It made a successful application to the Commerce Commission in December 2006, which ensured that 2007 was considered an exceptional year for the salary cap rules of the Air New Zealand Cup, instituted in 2006. It is interesting that the Commerce Commission considered it exceptional when they had only instituted the rule six months before.

Most New Zealand rugby fans will also hope 2007 was exceptional, in the same way that Robbie Deans doesn't want a repeat of what he went through. Unless something changes within the system, however, there is no assurance that it won't be repeated again, so powerful is the obsession that has developed in New Zealand to win the World Cup.

The Journey Begins

Rotation, conditioning, flat backlines and poor lineouts have been the features of many discussions about Henry's All Blacks. Despite all the criticisms, the All Blacks have only been beaten five times in forty-three tests in the lead-up to the 2007 World Cup. Any other country would be raving about such a record. In New Zealand it is expected.

- Why has it been so difficult to replace Umaga?

- Who is to blame for the lineout shambles?

- Has rotation stopped the development of combinations?

- Is conditioning something that should only happen to cars?

ALTHOUGH THERE HAVE BEEN many issues raised and discussed throughout the time Henry has been coaching the All Blacks, the issues of rotation, lineouts and flat backlines have dominated. In the pre-match and post-match discussions surrounding the games, these were the topics the press and the fans belaboured. Any respectable analysis of All Black teams during the Henry era must highlight his 'rotation' of players — a term foreign to rugby until 2004; before then, if a player missed selection he was simply 'dropped'.

The idea behind rotation was to develop a squad with genuine depth, with at least two players able to play at test level in any one position. The theory was that the All Blacks would be able to replace any player injured without the team's performance being adversely affected. Henry was at pains to point out that rugby was no longer a fifteen-man game. Ever since the replacement rules had come into test rugby, results were often determined by the coach who made the best use of his bench. This had been hard enough for the purists to take on board, but now they were being asked to accept that the best players in some positions wouldn't even be in the twenty-two-man squad.

> Ever since the replacement rules had come into test rugby, results were often determined by the coach who made the best use of his bench.

The reaction from the heartland was as quick as it was predictable. 'The black jersey is being cheapened,' they thundered on talkback. Some pointed out that Henry would never establish combinations and continuity if players were constantly being changed. Others highlighted the fact that key players like McCaw and Carter weren't being spelled.

Henry's reaction to the constant questioning was interesting. Initially he tried to sell the policy by explaining its purpose carefully.

This didn't please people, and the coach became grumpy and short-tempered with those who persisted in questioning the policy. Normally he handles the media well, but this became more like a headmaster telling off a group of errant third-formers than the All Black coach getting the national media onside.

The consistent failure of All Black packs to win their own lineout ball has been matched by their inability to challenge the opposition's ball. It is inexcusable that a group of such natural athletes can stuff up such a simple job. Some of the attempts to rectify the lineout woes were verging on comical, as 'pods' of players ran up and down the lineout doing a reasonable imitation of an elongated Charlie Chaplin and the Keystone Cops. At times the throwers were ridiculed, with Anton Oliver receiving more than his fair share of the blame. On other occasions the jumpers and the lifters became the target of fans' displeasure.

The person who avoided criticism the longest was Steve Hansen, whose responsibility it was to make the lineout work. Shortly after the media blowtorch was turned on Hansen, former All Black lock Robin Brooke was called in to assist. His message was a simple one — back to basics — with immediate results. The question remains why Hansen hadn't been able to fix it on his own.

The person who avoided criticism the longest was Steve Hansen, whose responsibility it was to make the lineout work.

Henry hasn't tried to explain the flat backline for some time. He's been coaching it now for over thirty years. Questions directed to him on it are greeted with a silent disdain — in fact you can see him mentally categorizing the questioner as a 'rugby nitwit'.

The flat backline is even more essential now with all the emphasis on getting over the advantage line. A deep backline is nullified by drift defence and ends up over the sideline.

Despite this, there have been times when some of his backs have struggled to put passes in front of the receiver in the flat formation. The argument that the backs would be better on attack if they were deeper is one Henry dismissed while coaching Auckland Grammar all those years ago.

The flat backline is even more essential now with all the emphasis on getting over the advantage line. A deep backline is nullified by drift defence and ends up over the sideline. In Dan Carter and Nick Evans, the coach has two first five-eighths adept at taking the ball to the line. The big advantage of a flat formation is that if you do break through, you're *right* through, with the cover defence having no time to make the tackle.

What the questioners *should* have been posing to the coach was why the All Black backline wasn't a little deeper at set pieces. After all, we've seen Pacific Island teams successfully use a deeper formation at set play, with players running hard and flat onto the ball.

FOR THE RECORD

What was Henry's record as All Black coach, where every match played can now be seen as a vital step on that crucial four-year journey to the 2007 World Cup? Let the record speak for itself.

Here is how it played on the field in the first three years.

WIN	LOSS
1	–

Date   12 June 2004
Venue   Dunedin
Against   England
Score   36 – 3

Significant factors

Henry couldn't have hoped for a better way to start his coaching tenure with the All Blacks. The convincing win against England not only helped to erase the painful memories of the 2003 World Cup, but also helped create the impression that he and his new selection panel could install a brand of rugby that would not only bring victories but entertain the fans. On a personal level, such a convincing victory over Clive Woodward also gave Henry an early taste of the personal satisfaction he'd be able to derive from coaching a team with as much talent as the All Blacks.

Tana Umaga's selection as captain to replace Reuben Thorne was the feature selection of this first match. Things couldn't have gone better for Umaga, and the convincing result prepared the nation for two highly successful years with Henry leading off the field and Umaga on the field.

Henry settled on Carlos Spencer as the first-five — a player he'd always managed to get the best from — with Dan Carter at second-five and the number one goalkicker.

The recall of Carl Hayman, who hadn't donned the black jersey since the Welsh test in November 2002, was also significant. Hayman went on to become the cornerstone of the All Black scrum for the duration of Henry's campaign towards the 2007 World Cup. The other number-one prop pick for much of Henry's campaign, Tony Woodcock, also appeared off the bench for the first time since that Welsh test. Yet another significant selection was Keith Robinson, who also hadn't played since the Welsh test — he helped ensure the All Black tight five secured dominance over an English pack that had been expected to trouble them.

The most disputable selections came in the loose forwards, with Jono Gibbes making his debut and Xavier Rush filling the number 8 jersey that had been Jerry Collins' the year before. Both Gibbes and Rush more than justified their selections with top games. Gibbes, in particular, was outstanding in the air, bringing dominance to the lineouts and securing the English kick-offs. A 33-point advantage over the World Cup holders was a significant victory for a new All Black coach. He was on his way. However, the most significant aspect of this match was a head injury to Richie McCaw halfway through the second half, which kept him out of the entire 2004 Tri-Nations campaign.

WIN	LOSS		
2	—	Date	**19 June 2004**
		Venue	**Auckland**
		Against	**England**
		Score	**36 – 12**

Significant factors

If the first test was over at halftime, this match was effectively over after 10 minutes, when English lock Simon Shaw was sent from the field for kneeing Keith Robinson in the head at ruck time.

The English were able to hold the score to 10 – 6 at halftime, but the All Blacks ran away with it in the second half, Joe Rokocoko touching down three times and Carlos Spencer scoring once.

The absence of Richie McCaw and Doug Howlett, both due to

injuries, forced the only changes to the starting line-up from the first test. Nick Evans had made his test debut the previous week as a substitute on the wing, but this time was allowed to start in his preferred position of fullback, with Mils Muliaina shuffling out to Howlett's wing spot.

Carlos Spencer played the last quarter of the match at fullback, with Andrew Mehrtens coming on to play first-five, his first appearance under Graham Henry.

WIN	LOSS		
3	**–**	Date	26 June 2004
		Venue	Hamilton
		Against	Argentina
		Score	41 – 7

Significant factors

While the win was convincing enough on the scoreboard, post-match Henry described the performance as 'messy, a tough night at the office'. In part this was a credit to the pressure Argentina were able to place on the All Blacks throughout the match. He went on to say, 'I think we'll be better off for that, we've learned a bit about ourselves. Argentina played well and put a lot of pressure on us but there were some positives.'

This was also Henry's first look at a wider group of players — the most prominent being Byron Kelleher and Andrew Mehrtens, at numbers 9 and 10 respectively. It was a glimpse of what was to come, as Henry would be prepared to rest, rotate and experiment with players in test matches throughout his coaching reign.

Two significant changes were the inclusion of starting debuts for Sam Tuitupou and Mose Tuiali'i, who'd attended Kelston Boys' High School where Henry had been principal. Both scored tries, while a third Kelston boy, Mils Muliaina, also touched down as he continued to cover on the wing for the injured Doug Howlett.

Jerry Collins made his first start under Henry, and his selection on the blindside flank was very significant. John Mitchell had preferred to use him at number 8, but Henry clearly saw his skill-set was better suited to the number 6 jersey.

WIN	LOSS
4	–

Date   10 July 2004
Venue   Albany
Against   Pacific Islands
Score   41 – 26

Significant factors

This match was more notable for the glimpses of talent shown by Sitiveni Sivivatu and Sione Lauaki for the Pacific Islanders, than for anything from the All Blacks. While both these players displayed the raw ability they'd shown for the Chiefs during the Super 12, the overall All Black performance wasn't convincing. The knowledge that both Sivivatu and Lauaki were eligible for the All Blacks would have given Henry at least one positive to take out of the match.

The Fijian cousins Rokocoko and Sivivatu dominated in the try-scoring stakes, with two tries apiece for their respective teams.

Overall this was a disappointing display by the All Blacks, who were sucked into the Islanders' style of rugby, failing to do the hard yards up front before throwing the ball wide. This was a lesson Henry would have to remind his team of throughout his tenure as coach — that despite having talent to burn in the backline, the first priority should always be to set the platform up first.

WIN	LOSS
5	–

Date   17 July 2004
Venue   Wellington
Against   Australia
Score   16 – 7

Significant factors

Henry reverted to his first test line-up for this key Bledisloe Cup and Tri-Nations encounter, where a victory would retain the Bledisloe Cup. The match wasn't memorable — shocking conditions and a high penalty count dictated that it was a low-scoring, dour affair.

WIN	LOSS		
6	**–**	Date	24 July 2004
		Venue	Christchurch
		Against	South Africa
		Score	23 – 21

Significant factors

This was the first real test of Henry's coaching reign, and he was very lucky to retain his unbeaten run. After scoring in the first minute, South Africa led for most of the match and it was only a Doug Howlett try in the 79th minute that saved the match for the All Blacks, giving them a commanding lead in the Tri-Nations.

Henry showed a willingness to turn to his bench under pressure, with his side trailing 21 – 15 and 26 minutes still remaining — Ali Williams replaced Simon Maling. Nine minutes later and still 3 points down, Kelleher came on for Marshall and Tuitupou for Carter. The changes paid off, and the All Blacks were able to head offshore with two from two in the 2004 Tri-Nations.

However, a win is not always enough for All Black supporters, and growing criticism was forming in New Zealand of Henry's flat backline — particularly the way it had been shown up by the Springboks' rush defence. Backs coach Wayne Smith copped at least as much, if not more, criticism than Henry himself. Henry made it quite clear that the flat backline was here to stay.

'The philosophy is fine, what we're trying to do makes sense. The players want to do it, the coaches want to do it, and we think it's the right policy. We've just got to perfect it,' he said before leaving for the next Tri-Nations test in Australia.

WIN	LOSS
6	1

Date | 7 August 2004
Venue | Sydney
Against | Australia
Score | 18 – 23

Significant factors

Too many turnovers — particularly off their own ball into the lineout — were largely to blame for the All Blacks losing their first match under Henry. They were also punished by referee Jonathan Kaplan.

The match was also notable for the end of Carlos Spencer's international career. He was replaced by Andrew Mehrtens in the 50th minute, and for the following match would be dropped altogether from the twenty-two-man squad to take the field against South Africa. While Spencer wouldn't be seen again, the flat backline debate grew stronger in light of the All Blacks' first loss of the season.

WIN	LOSS
6	2

Date | 14 August 2004
Venue | Johannesburg
Against | South Africa
Score | 26 – 40

Significant factors

This test may be the most significant match of Henry's coaching career. It is often said that you learn more from your losses than your wins. In Johannesburg, Henry's All Blacks were convincingly beaten five tries to two, with centre Marius Joubert touching down for a hat-trick. The loss also meant that Australia and South Africa were left to battle for Tri-Nations glory the following week — a match that gave South Africa their first Tri-Nations crown.

More significantly, the loss prompted Henry to make changes in his squad for the four-match northern-hemisphere tour. Only eleven of the players named had been used during his eight tests in charge so far, with established players like Marshall, Mehrtens and Spencer effectively dropped.

WIN	LOSS
7	**2**

Date **13 November 2004**
Venue **Rome**
Against **Italy**
Score **59 – 10**

Significant factors

Dan Carter's selection at first-five was very quickly seen as much more than an experiment by Graham Henry. After Conrad Smith had scored with his first touch of the ball in an All Black jersey, Carter scored a classy individual try — chipping over the defence and catching the ball to run in for the All Blacks' second try, only five minutes into the match.

He continued to look at home in the number 10 jersey for the rest of the match. From a team perspective, the All Blacks took the foot off the throat in the second half after having the match effectively won at halftime courtesy of a 35 – 3 lead.

Enough positives were seen in the match to raise the spirit of disgruntled fans, and by its conclusion they were no longer talking flat backline — they were fascinated by the prospect of an All Black backline rejuvenated by the young genius of Carter.

WIN	LOSS
8	**2**

Date **20 November 2004**
Venue **Cardiff**
Against **Wales**
Score **26 – 25**

Significant factors

Tana Umaga was rested, and Richie McCaw's first test as captain nearly turned into a disaster — more the result of a stunning performance by the Welsh than the All Blacks struggling with unfamiliar combinations.

The sin-binning of replacement mid-fielder Ma'a Nonu for a late hit on Gavin Henson didn't help, as things remained tight in the last quarter.

In the end, Welsh captain Gareth Thomas's decision to opt for a kick at goal with four minutes to go, rather than kick the ball out and attack the All Blacks' line, saved them; the All Blacks maintained their 1-point lead through to the final whistle.

WIN	LOSS		
9	**2**	Date	27 November 2004
		Venue	Paris
		Against	France
		Score	45 – 6

Significant factors

This was an important victory for the All Blacks — the biggest ever by an All Black team in France, against the reigning Six Nations champions.

> **New Zealand rugby purists will always remember this test for ending any claim of French superiority at scrum time.**

The loose-forward trio of Collins, McCaw and So'oialo at 6, 7 and 8 respectively proved to Henry they could work together effectively as a unit and give the All Blacks a crucial edge around the field. All three had outstanding games, and the platform they provided also meant Byron Kelleher had one of his best games as an All Black, claiming the official man-of-the-match title.

New Zealand rugby purists will always remember this test for ending any claim of French superiority at scrum time. The French were humiliated, claimed they had no more fit props, and demanded 'Golden Oldies' scrums for the rest of the game. The expression on Anton Oliver's face was priceless, and completely summed up the moment.

Dan Carter's 25-point personal tally and his control of the match merely reconfirmed what had been apparent in the previous two matches — he was destined for a long career in the All Blacks at first five-eighth, and this tour had been the perfect time for Henry to blood him.

WIN	LOSS
10	**2**

Date **4 December 2004**
Venue **London**
Against **Barbarians**
Score **47 – 19**

Significant factors

Henry used this match to start players who hadn't had much game time on tour. Most notably, Jerome Kaino had a top game in his debut for the All Blacks. The experimentation also meant Aaron Mauger captained the All Blacks for the first time and played the full match at first-five.

Dan Carter was wrapped up in cotton wool on the bench, in a match where the Barbarians looked too disjointed to seriously threaten the All Blacks.

WIN	LOSS
11	**2**

Date   **10 June 2005**
Venue   **Albany**
Against **Fiji**
Score   **91 – 0**

Significant factors

At the time, most critics were reluctant to praise this stunning performance by the All Blacks, despite the fact that the Fijians had put up such a strong fight against the New Zealand Maori in Suva the previous week, only just losing 29 – 27 in a tight game. Hindsight now tells us this magnificent display of running rugby by Henry's men was something we'd get used to in the weeks that followed, when the Lions series kicked off.

A feature of the annihilation of the Fijians was the four tries on debut to Sitiveni Sivivatu against his fellow countrymen, one year after he'd played on the same ground as part of the Pacific Islands team. It was a world record for tries on debut, but only lasted 36 hours before South African wing Tonderai Chavanga touched down six times against Uruguay.

Sione Lauaki, who played a full half off the bench, was in the same boat as Sivivatu — also playing both for and against the All Blacks within twelve months. Lauaki was yet another All Black from Kelston Boys' High School.

WIN	LOSS
12	**2**

Date   **25 June 2005**
Venue   **Christchurch**
Against **Lions**
Score   **21 – 3**

Significant factors

The Lions have always been popular tourists. Traditionally they have played an open, exciting brand of rugby, very different from

162

the standard fare dished up by the individual countries making up the team. Many rate the 1971 Lions team that included outstanding backs like Gareth Edwards, Barry John, Mike Gibson, John Dawes, David Duckham, T.G.R. Davies and J.P.R. Williams as the best team to visit New Zealand since World War II.

It quickly became obvious that one of the most eagerly awaited series in All Black history could well turn into an anticlimax.

Whether or not you agree with this, one thing is for certain — the Lions have brought some magnificent players here, players who became household names from North Cape to the Bluff: Roger Spong and George Beamish in the 1930 team that lost the series one game to three; Jack Kyle and Ken Jones from the 1950 side; Tony O'Reilly and Peter Jackson from 1959; Jim Telfer and Willie John McBride from 1966; take your pick from the team line-up in 1971; Phil Bennett and Derek Quinell in 1977; Graham Price and Ollie Campbell from 1983; Gavin Hastings and Jeremy Guscott from 1993 — just some of the Lions players who were worshipped in a country where rugby is the national religion.

It quickly became obvious that one of the most eagerly awaited series in All Black history could well turn into an anticlimax — largely because of the many weaknesses within the Lions camp, but also because of the way Henry's All Blacks were starting to take shape in his second year in the job. Justin Marshall's experience meant he pipped Byron Kelleher for the disputed number 9 jersey, while Leon MacDonald kept Mils Muliaina on the bench, despite Mils later becoming one of Henry's first picks closer to the Cup. Ali Williams turned on a man-of-the-match performance that confirmed he'd matured sufficiently to be another player who would be important at the 2007 World Cup.

The fear going into the match that the All Blacks might be

bettered up-front quickly evaporated. In particular, ten lineout wins against the throw to the All Blacks meant the Lions never got enough possession to be competitive. Squally rain and hail kept the All Blacks from taking as much advantage of their dominance of possession as they might otherwise have been able to; there would be no such obstacle to save the Lions a week later in Wellington.

Looking back, the impact of the Lions losing both Dallaglio in their first match and O'Driscoll two minutes into the first test on the one-sided nature of this historic tour cannot be underestimated. It could probably be compared to the All Blacks losing Carter and McCaw, although the Lions' lack of depth may have made it even tougher for them. However, that would scarcely diminish the personal triumph Henry would have felt over Clive Woodward after this first victory, or the even greater feeling he'd enjoy when the All Blacks completed a clean sweep a fortnight later.

WIN	LOSS		
13	2		

Date	2 July 2005
Venue	Wellington
Against	Lions
Score	48 – 18

Significant factors

To many, this match will be remembered as the 'Dan Carter Show'. It may have also been the day those in the northern hemisphere woke up to the fact that Carter could be as influential in Henry's 2007 World Cup campaign as Jonny Wilkinson had been in Woodward's 2003 campaign. His four conversions, five penalty goals and two tries gave him a personal tally of 33 points for the match — a record by any player against the Lions.

After Gareth Thomas gave the Lions a dream start, the All Blacks slowly but surely began to apply pressure. With a score of 21 – 13 down at halftime, the tourists would have considered themselves still in the match, but as the second half progressed, Dan Carter and the All Blacks stamped their mark on the game, totally outclassing the visitors.

WIN	LOSS		
14	**2**	Date	9 July 2005
		Venue	Auckland
		Against	Lions
		Score	38 – 19

Significant factors

With the series won, Henry and his fellow selectors took this opportunity to blood players in some key positions. The most significant change came due to injury, with Luke McAlister starting at first-five in the place of Carter.

Other key changes included Rodney So'oialo starting at openside flanker — an indication that Henry was keen to experiment with options other than the reliable Marty Holah as a back-up for Richie McCaw.

Sione Lauaki also started his first test match at number 8, with some tipping him to threaten So'oialo for the starting position at the World Cup due to his more abrasive ability to create go-forward ball off the back of the scrum. However, the ongoing issue of Lauaki carrying too much weight and questions over his match fitness would continue to be his biggest barriers to establishing a regular spot in the All Black squad. Unfortunately for Lauaki, an injury late in the first half saw the more conservative back row of Collins, Holah and So'oialo take the field for the second half.

Holah's fresh legs did a world of good when Jerry Collins found himself sin-binned in the 54th minute, following in the footsteps of his Wellington team-mate Tana Umaga who was binned only seven minutes into the match. The Umaga decision failed to affect the All Blacks, who went on to score 14 unanswered points while he was off the field. Once he was back on, Umaga capped off a memorable series with two tries. McAlister's performance at first five-eighth raised hopes for the fans of another back-up for Carter.

Unlike Umaga's, Collins' sin-binning upset the flow for the All Blacks, but Rico Gear's intercept try in the last minute of the match gave a timely reminder of what one-way traffic the series had been.

It had been twelve years since the Lions had last played in New Zealand, and fans were heartily sick of the repetitive annual Tri-Nations series. The last time the Lions were in the South Pacific they had been coached by one G.W. Henry and had just failed to win a controversial series.

Austin Healey and Matt Dawson, two English players, wrote articles during the tour that were critical of Henry. Later English coach Clive Woodward wrote in the *Daily Mail* that:

> The highest standards have not been put forward by the Lions management from the start of this trip. They have not set the right example themselves. It is totally wrong for Graham Henry to be writing a book. If Matt or Austin had done this in the England set-up, they could only expect one result. However, if you do not set high standards at the top in this area, how can you expect the players to follow?

England's victory at the 2003 World Cup, combined with Woodward's subsequent knighthood, combined to leave New Zealand rugby supporters in desperate need of revenge. The lack of credible tours in the modern game also heightened anticipation of the Lions' arrival. By the time Woodward's men touched down in Auckland, there was a feeling similar to that experienced in 1956 before the legendary Springbok tour.

The last time the Lions were in the South Pacific they had been coached by one G.W. Henry and had just failed to win a controversial series.

It didn't help that the Lions closeted themselves in Bunker Hilton, probably the most expensive and palatial hotel in the country. From there they ventured out reluctantly into the provinces, where grass-roots New Zealand — who had been waiting desperately to embrace them — now felt jilted and wanted to see them slaughtered. Woodward was increasingly viewed as an arrogant snob looking down his nose at the ignorant colonials.

The bad guy had been clearly established. All Graham Henry had to do was win the series to become New Zealand rugby's equivalent of Superman. In truth, after the injuries to Dallaglio and O'Driscoll coupled with the mistakes Woodward made, *Helen Clark* could have coached the All Blacks to a series victory.

WIN	LOSS
14	3

Date   6 August 2005
Venue   Capetown
Against South Africa
Score   16 – 22

Significant factors

Sport is a great leveller, and after the euphoria associated with victory over the Lions the old foe South Africa ambushed the All Blacks at Capetown. The error-count read 15 – 4 against the All Blacks, with mistakes coming largely as the result of extreme pressure by the South Africans through their rush defence and their targeting of the New Zealand lineout. Once again Henry's critics questioned his use of the flat backline.

In particular the pressure told in the early minutes of the match, as the Africans took a 13 – 0 lead after only fifteen minutes. Dan

Carter had a poor game by his own high standards — a timely reminder for New Zealand supporters that he was human after all.

Carter may have been upset by more than just South Africa's pressure. He also lost his starting halfback, Byron Kelleher, only ten minutes into the match. Kelleher's injury moved former South African halfback Kevin Putt to raise some controversy over a concealed plate in Springbok lock Victor Matfield's arm on the Sky TV show *Deaker on Sport*, his comments raising a storm of protest in South Africa.

Kelleher's replacement, Piri Weepu, handled himself well considering it was only his second test match appearance. But good individual performances weren't enough to counter the constant mistakes Henry's men made from start to finish. From a South African perspective, the match provided a clear-cut blueprint on how to beat the All Blacks — pressure, pressure and more pressure.

Good individual performances weren't enough to counter the constant mistakes Henry's men made from start to finish.

The South Africans have always treasured the opportunity to play the All Blacks and the results between the two countries have usually been close. Until the Springboks were isolated from international competition by their country's policy of apartheid, their record against the All Blacks was approximately 50 per cent success, much better than any other nation. That tradition has been engrained in their players, with Springbok teams really believing they can beat the All Blacks. No other nation consistently shows the same self-belief against the men in black. The biggest challenge the All Blacks would continue to face from South Africa, right through to the World Cup, would be matching not only that self-belief but also the passion and intensity the Boks bring to their games against them.

WIN	LOSS	Date	13 August 2005
15	**3**	Venue	**Sydney**
		Against	**Australia**
		Score	**30 – 13**

Significant factors

For the second week in a row, the All Blacks found themselves down by 13 points to nil early in the match. This time, however, they then managed to pile up 30 unanswered points against the Australians. The convincing win came despite the fact that, for the second week in a row, the All Black lineout was shocking.

Forwards coach Steve Hansen came under fire from the New Zealand media and public for his inability to rectify the situation. The problem would continue to linger for the next year, and became one of the major obstacles to Henry's teams obtaining complete domination over their opponents.

With fifteen minutes to go, the match was still in the balance at 16 – 13 when Richie McCaw showed the type of leadership that would see him go on to succeed Tana Umaga as captain the following year. Spotting the Australian defenders slightly on their heels, McCaw tapped a penalty 5 metres out and ran over three defenders to score. The buffer created by this converted try became a blessing for the All Blacks four minutes later when their other great asset, Carter, sustained what would later be diagnosed as a broken leg.

WIN	LOSS	Date	27 August 2005
16	**3**	Venue	**Dunedin**
		Against	**South Africa**
		Score	**31 – 27**

Significant factors

This was a thrilling match where the lead changed hands numerous times, highlighting the fact that South Africa was indeed the hardest team for the All Blacks to beat.

Leon MacDonald was handed the crucial number 10 jersey in Dan Carter's absence, despite McAlister's convincing display in the third test against the Lions. At the time Henry justified the decision by explaining what good form MacDonald was in. 'Leon played exceptionally well for Canterbury at the weekend. We also looked at the combination between 9 and 10 and felt it was better to opt for experience.'

Following an average performance by MacDonald, McAlister took over with his team trailing 27 – 24 and only eleven minutes to go. The move paid off for Henry, but the question still remained as to why MacDonald had been there in the first place. Playing MacDonald at centre in 2003's semi-final loss to Australia was bad enough — surely they wouldn't use him in a crucial match at first-five in 2007 if Carter was injured?

The winning try came from Keven Mealamu with four minutes of the match remaining, and capped off an outstanding game for him. The game also marked a return to form for Joe Rokocoko, who up until then had been struggling to find the type of try-scoring form he'd quickly become renowned for since arriving on the international scene two years before.

WIN	LOSS		
17	**3**		

Date	3 September 2005
Venue	Auckland
Against	Australia
Score	34 – 24

Significant factors

The All Blacks seemed to have total control early in this match, leading 20 – 0 after only thirty minutes. In a stunning turnaround Australia hit back, and over the next twenty minutes were able to post 19 unanswered points, led by some great individual play from Mark Gerrard and a sharp performance by Mat Rogers in the number 10 jersey.

The last of Australia's 19-point resurgence came as a Leon MacDonald kick was charged down for the second time in consecutive matches. Again, why he started in the first place remains a mystery and it wasn't long before he was replaced. Luke McAlister came on eight minutes into the second half, nailing three penalties in quick succession.

Byron Kelleher went off injured late in the match, which allowed for Kevin Senio to make his test debut. The last All Black score came with Doug Howlett touching down for his first test match hat-trick in the dying minutes of the match, securing the Tri-Nations for the 2005 All Blacks.

WIN	LOSS		
18	**3**		

Date	5 November 2005
Venue	Cardiff
Against	Wales
Score	41 – 3

Significant factors

Intent on building depth within his squad on this tour, Henry named a large squad of thirty-five, including five uncapped players: Isaia Toeava, Jason Eaton, Chris Masoe, Angus MacDonald and Neemia Tialata. Henry started Masoe and Tialata in their test debuts against the Welsh and gave MacDonald fifteen minutes off the bench late in the second half.

Though McCaw came on for Masoe for the last twelve minutes, it was encouraging for Henry to see such a dominant All Black display without one of his two key superstars. His other star, Dan Carter, couldn't have had a better return to test rugby, notching up 26 points in his first match since breaking his leg in the Tri-Nations.

The only other All Black to get on the scoreboard was Rico Gear, who notched up a hat-trick of tries.

WIN	LOSS
19	**3**

Date   **12 November 2005**
Venue   **Dublin**
Against   **Ireland**
Score   **45 – 7**

Significant factors

Sticking firmly to his word about trying to develop two competent test players in each position building towards the 2007 World Cup, Henry made fifteen selection changes for this match. Despite playing without first-stringers Tana Umaga, Daniel Carter, Jerry Collins and Carl Hayman, Henry was still able to field world-class wingers in Sitiveni Sivivatu and Doug Howlett, who both scored two tries. Jason Eaton and John Afoa both also started in their debuts for the All Blacks.

Richie McCaw returned to the starting line-up, captaining the All Blacks for only the second time. Apart from the captain, this team was viewed largely as an All Black B team. They looked far from it, though, turning in a classy performance with good continuity considering how little the players had played together. It justified Henry's decision to take such a large squad, to enable the so-called B team to train together while the 'other' test team prepared for their match against Wales.

This match was also significant as the first time Nick Evans started a match at first five-eighth for the All Blacks. His convincing display meant he was now viewed as another player who could attempt to fill Carter's boots.

WIN	LOSS
20	**3**

Date   **19 November 2005**
Venue   **London**
Against   **England**
Score   **23 – 19**

Significant factors

England dominated the early part of this match, scoring after only five minutes. The All Blacks started very poorly — their skill level, coordination and teamwork well below the expected standard. Despite that, by halftime the All Blacks had fought back to take a 13 – 10 lead.

England put up much more of a fight than expected, but the All Blacks' defensive patterns stood up when it counted. However, the pressure did see Woodcock, Tialata and Masoe sent to the sin-bin by Irish referee Alan Lewis, for professional fouls. At one stage the men in black were down to thirteen players.

Dan Carter was again a shining light, setting up tries for Keven Mealamu and Tana Umaga.

WIN	LOSS		
21	**3**	Date	**26 November 2005**
		Venue	**Edinburgh**
		Against	**Scotland**
		Score	**29 – 10**

Significant factors

Despite the prospect of winning only New Zealand's second-ever Grand Slam over the Home Nations, Henry wasn't afraid to look at the bigger picture and make massive changes to further grow the base of players he was developing in his run towards the 2007 World Cup.

This meant twelve changes to the team from the previous week, with only Richie McCaw, Chris Jack and Tana Umaga starting both weeks in a row. Nick Evans got another chance to prove himself as the first-five best equipped to be Dan Carter's back-up, while Isaia Toeava debuted, becoming the youngest All Black to play against Scotland.

The match itself threatened to turn into one-way traffic when the All Blacks led 22 – 3 at halftime. However, a spirited effort from the Scots saw the second half result in a converted try apiece. This loss of All Black momentum wasn't helped by Henry's willingness to give all twenty-two players a run, even at the cost of continuity.

Who could argue with this? While many of the big matches had been close, Henry had managed to see out 2005 with only one loss from eleven test matches. Just as importantly, he'd created a larger pool of players he was confident of using in test matches, and his players' confidence in him and his fellow selectors' was starting to grow.

WIN	LOSS		
22	**3**	Date	10 June 2006
		Venue	Hamilton
		Against	Ireland
		Score	34 – 23

Significant factors

If Graham Henry's decision to play two different starting teams in two weeks in November 2005 had indicated he wasn't afraid to do things differently, the decisions he took at the beginning of 2006 confirmed it. While he named a squad of thirty-nine, fifteen of them sat out the two Irish tests in New Zealand and were sent over to Argentina early, to acclimatize.

After only forty-three seconds of this first match against Ireland Doug Howlett touched down, finishing off a break-out from his own 22 by Mils Muliaina. The Irish fought back, helped largely by the All Black lineout problems that came back to haunt them from the previous year. By halftime the Irish were right back into the match and led 16 – 8, and if they had taken their chances or had slightly more strike power out wide, they might have been able to steal a victory.

Eventually the All Blacks' class came through. Troy Flavell touched down in the 73rd minute to seal the match after coming on for the last half-hour to replace South-African-born debutant Greg Rawlinson. Both were players who might not have had the opportunity to prove themselves if it wasn't for Henry's rotation system.

Flavell's raw talent, his intimidating style and his ability to play lock and blindside were the qualities that encouraged Henry to entice the controversial West Aucklander back from Japan. Although the selection panel had shown a preference for specialists, Flavell's ability to play well in two troubling positions for the All Blacks made him a real World Cup prospect.

Much of the interest for this first test of the year focused on how the mid-field would go without Tana Umaga. Ma'a Nonu was given a prime opportunity to stake his claim for the position, as he was paired up with the second-five Aaron Mauger. However, Nonu's performance was unconvincing and he came in for the same type of criticism his career had been plagued by, with a defensive lapse leading to Ireland's first try, and a series of turnovers providing justification for this criticism.

The experimentation of playing specialist openside Marty Holah on the blindside was another failure. He had a prime opportunity, playing with McCaw and So'oialo, but the All Blacks seemed to really miss a ball-runner getting over the advantage line within the loose-forward trio.

WIN	LOSS		
23	**3**	Date	17 June 2006
		Venue	Auckland
		Against	Ireland
		Score	27 – 17

Significant factors

The All Blacks were again pushed hard by the Irish, but unfortunately their willingness to keep the ball in play didn't suit the atrocious conditions. Just as they had done in the previous week, the Irish successfully targeted the All Blacks' lineout, giving incentive for

Ronan O'Gara to put the ball out and direct a territorially oriented game for the Irish. In contrast the All Blacks played too much rugby in their own half and, despite his reliable goal-kicking, some of McAlister's choices showed his inexperience.

Debutant David Hill replaced McAlister for the last six minutes at first-five, highlighting the lack of depth within the squad in that position. Henry had to put up with the frustration of having Nick Evans out for the home season with a shoulder injury sustained in Super 14 play.

The two tests had shown that if the All Blacks met Ireland at the World Cup, they would need to be right on the job or they could be given a fright — just like the 1991 Wallabies.

WIN	LOSS
24	3

Date   **24 June 2006**
Venue   **Buenos Aires**
Against   **Argentina**
Score   **25 – 19**

Significant factors

Henry's appointment of Jerry Collins as captain for this test raised many eyebrows, especially with former captain Anton Oliver down to start the match. More than anything, it emphasized how Collins was now viewed as one of five certain picks within Henry's squad, and just how far the enforcer's game had developed. The match was dominated by the whistle of English referee Nigel Whitehouse, who ensured there was very little flow, and the All Blacks never gained momentum.

An off-night with the boot for Dan Carter didn't help, although slippery conditions and a knock he took during the second half could both explain his uncharacteristic inaccuracy.

Much interest surrounded Isaia Toeava's first start at centre for the All Blacks, but due to the stop-start nature of the match, very little could be read into his performance. Scott Hamilton was rewarded for some outstanding Super 14 form with a starting position on the left wing, from where he touched down for the All Blacks' second try.

A great test of the All Black defence came in the final minutes of the match when the Argentinians were hot on attack and Leon MacDonald was in the sin-bin. The Pumas put phase after phase together, as they attempted to bash their way through the fourteen-man All Black wall. Despite so many changes from the previous test, the New Zealanders displayed good organization and confidence in their defence as they held on for the victory.

WIN	LOSS		
25	**3**		

Date   **8 July 2006**
Venue   **Christchurch**
Against   **Australia**
Score   **32 – 12**

Significant factors

All season, much of the talk had been about how Henry would best replace Tana Umaga at centre for matches that really mattered. Picking his first number-one side in 2006, Henry answered this question by selecting Leon MacDonald at fullback and moving Mils Muliaina to centre, a broken thumb sustained by Ma'a Nonu limiting his selection options.

The match itself was a brilliant spectacle, both sides showing a willingness to move the ball in conditions suited to open rugby. The turning point was undoubtedly a yellow card in the 27th minute to Rocky Elsom for constant infringements. By the time he returned from the bin the Australians had gone from 7 – 0 up to 14 – 7 down.

From there, a strong All Black forward display enabled Henry's men to take control of the match. Isaia Toeava sealed it for them when he scored his first try in the black jersey with four minutes to go. While the match was memorable itself, many will remember this as the day Jerry Collins elected to relieve himself on the field just before the game.

WIN	LOSS
26	**3**

Date   22 July 2006
Venue   Wellington
Against   South Africa
Score   35 – 17

Significant factors

Henry again showed a willingness to rotate players, making eight changes from what had been considered his number-one side the week before, and the All Blacks had a poor start. Dan Carter had a kick charged down by Fourie du Preez minutes into the match, and the Springboks took an early lead.

Though they soon bounced back, the All Black performance was patchy, hindered by the old lineout problems that ensured they never took full control of the match. In the end their comfortable win was largely due to Dan Carter turning in a performance nearly as good as the one he'd displayed at the same ground against the Lions the year before, ending the match with 25 points to his name.

WIN	LOSS
27	**3**

Date   29 July 2006
Venue   Sydney
Against   Australia
Score   13 – 9

Significant factors

At the end of the season Graham Henry looked back on this game as the year's most satisfying victory. It wasn't because it meant the Bledisloe Cup was retained — it was the *way* it was retained. The All Blacks showed tremendous spirit in defence in a match where they dominated the scrums and breakdown, but struggled with possession due to problems yet again at lineout time.

Richie McCaw turned in a memorable performance that day even by his own high standards, his effort moving Henry to state after the match, 'You can't play better than that.'

Opposition wing Mark Gerrard, pulled down in a try-saving tackle in the second half by McCaw, also heaped praise on the All Black captain, saying, 'He's anywhere and everywhere, it seemed like we were playing four or five of him.'

WIN	LOSS		
28	**3**	Date	19 August 2006
		Venue	Auckland
		Against	Australia
		Score	34 – 27

Significant factors

After taking the conservative option of Muliaina at centre and MacDonald at fullback for the early matches in the Tri-Nations, Henry decided to give Isaia Toeava his first test start at centre. Toeava struggled in the role, and after going into halftime 20 – 11 down Henry reverted back to the combination used in previous games.

The value of Henry's rotation system was seen when Aaron Mauger injured his ankle pre-match, allowing Luke McAlister to step into the position. McAlister handled the challenge well. A further example happened twenty-six minutes into the match, when the rock of the All Black scrum, Carl Hayman, was forced from the field, leaving Greg Somerville to play over two-thirds of the match from the bench.

Lote Tuqiri scored from an intercepted Jerry Collins pass during a first half when nothing went the All Blacks' way, but a couple of Dan Carter penalties helped to close the gap as the All Blacks worked their way back into the match after halftime. Tries followed later on to Chris Jack and Luke McAlister, as an improved lineout performance paid dividends and All Black scrum dominance proved decisive.

It was a far from perfect All Black performance, but once again Henry's team had done the job. Two matches in South Africa still remained, but they had already claimed the Tri-Nations.

WIN	LOSS
29	**3**

Date   26 August 2006
Venue   Pretoria
Against   South Africa
Score   45 – 26

Significant factors

This was Henry's first win in South Africa, and although the final result was very convincing his team struggled to gain momentum and continuity for much of the first half. The All Blacks' inability to get going may have been the result of the eleven changes he made for the match, with both Leon MacDonald and Greg Somerville having to be replaced in the first quarter due to injuries.

The messy nature of the game played into the All Blacks' hands, with their superior ability to attack from anywhere coming to the fore in the second half. But yet again the All Black lineout woes returned, highlighting what remained a major problem.

The match provided a prime example of how Henry's rotation system had been so successful, yet could still prove fallible.

Probably the most memorable part of the match came just before halftime when Dan Carter kicked a 61-metre penalty, the longest 3-pointer by an All Black this century. Henry's other star player, Richie McCaw, appeared to be targeted by the South Africans at the kickoffs and Henry promised post-match to take his concerns to the IRB following the Tri-Nations.

The match provided a prime example of how Henry's rotation system had been so successful, yet could still prove fallible. Quite simply, Richie McCaw and Dan Carter were head and shoulders above their opposites in two key areas of the game — McCaw's clinical work at the breakdown and Carter's general ability to control the direction of the game giving the All Blacks a significant edge. The other thirteen players Henry fielded on this particular day were largely irrelevant, so long as they did the basics and brought to the field the X-factor provided by many of New Zealand's top Polynesian players.

After the match, South African coach Jake White alluded to the value of Carter and McCaw when he said, 'I really wouldn't mind if they'd give the number 7 and number 10 jerseys to someone else sometime.' White's cynical words spoke volumes.

White also felt that the absence through injury of 'Bakkies' Botha, Schalk Burger and Juan Smith had taken its toll on his team's defensive strategy and alignment. Those who watched the way his troops struggled to defend in the second half of the game would have to agree.

WIN	LOSS
29	**4**

Date   **2 September 2006**
Venue   **Rustenburg**
Against   **South Africa**
Score   **20 – 21**

Significant factors

The temptation to rest McCaw or Carter for this match was resisted and the expectation was that the All Blacks would complete their clean sweep of the Tri-Nations. However, the Springboks played with tremendous passion and determination, winning a critical test.

More significant than the All Blacks loss was the impact it had on the coaching career of Henry's opposite, Jake White. Having lost five matches on the trot going into this test, White's head was on the chopping block. If he'd been cut so close to the World Cup it could have spelt disaster for the South Africans. Instead, this victory provided the impetus for White to turn around not only his own career, but also to establish South Africa as a real threat at the 2007 World Cup. This cannot be overemphasized.

The match also marked the day Rodney So'oialo had such a nightmare of a game that if it hadn't been for the great faith Henry had in his number 8 he would have been dropped for the end-of-year tour. So'oialo was involved in three key plays during the game, the most prominent coming with two minutes to go when he gave away a match-winning penalty by taking out Victor Matfield from the side of a maul.

This victory provided the impetus for coach Jake White to turn around not only his own career, but also to establish South Africa as a real threat at the 2007 World Cup.

Earlier So'oialo had kept South Africa in the match twice in the first half. First came a loopy pass to Aaron Mauger on his 22 which the intercept king, Bryan Habana, gratefully accepted. The other came through less obvious circumstances when he cost Andrew Hore a try, the video referee claiming So'oialo had taken out the players ahead of him. If he'd had better cover on the bench Henry might have replaced So'oialo at halftime, it was so apparent that it just wasn't his day.

So'oialo was only part of the problem. He couldn't be blamed for the continuation of the All Black lineout woes and a performance that lacked intensity. This led to criticism of the All Blacks' match preparation. The players had spent much of the week leading into the test at the Sun City Resort, where it appeared to many that they were more worried about their tans and their golf games than getting ready for a test. As a result, the All Blacks missed a golden opportunity to end Jake White's career and humiliate South African rugby.

WIN	LOSS
30	**4**

Date   5 November 2006
Venue   London
Against   England
Score   41 – 10

Significant factors

At halftime in this match you could easily be left with the impression that Henry's All Blacks had spent the two months since their loss to South Africa waiting for a chance to redeem themselves. By halftime the All Blacks were up 28 – 5, a wonderful first half for a team that hadn't played any warm-up matches.

Henry chose to go with what would largely be considered his number-one line-up for this first match on tour, his strangest decision being in the loose forwards where Masoe and Thorne started ahead of So'oialo and Collins.

England weren't so blessed with their selection options, with injury taking its toll on a large number of their premium players. To their credit, they also attempted to play a better brand of rugby than most English teams have over recent years. They were also very unlucky to have Jamie Noon's try in the first five minutes denied by the referee when common sense suggested he had scored. The disallowed try meant the All Blacks were able to establish total control by halftime.

Keith Robinson's return to the team brought with it an encouraging improvement in the All Blacks' performance at lineout. The match was always safe, and provided Henry with the opportunity to debut Andrew Ellis off the bench and give Clarke Dermody and John Afoa rare opportunities to play.

Second-half momentum was hindered when Chris Masoe was unlucky to receive a yellow card for not rolling away in the tackle when in reality he was pinned at the bottom of a ruck by Ben Cohen. It was even more unfortunate that Masoe was beginning to really get onto his game at the time.

WIN	LOSS
31	4

Date   **11 November 2006**
Venue   Lyon
Against   France
Score   **47 – 3**

Significant factors

The old adage that you never know which French team will turn up was never more apparent than in this test, where the French seemed to lie down and let Graham Henry's team run in seven tries in a record-breaking victory.

Henry made ten changes from the previous week, although the number was beginning to mean little because of the minimal difference between players in many positions. It was clear from the selection of Dan Carter, along with the inclusion of the best loose-forward trio together with the top two props, that the All Black coach had real respect for the opposition.

Conrad Smith's first start for some time was also significant, and Henry pairing Smith with McAlister at second-five possibly indicated an eye to the future.

Considering the wet conditions, Henry could hardly have asked for more from his men. Notwithstanding the result, with his experience he would have left the match fully aware that a much more competitive French team might turn up at the World Cup in just under a year's time; and even the following week, as the teams moved to Paris.

WIN	LOSS
32	4

Date   **18 November 2006**
Venue   Paris
Against   France
Score   **23 – 11**

Significant factors

As if predicting the French resistance would be tougher, Henry picked the team he labelled 'the best right now' for this match. Translated for the couch potato, this meant he was playing what he considered to be his number-one team. The features of this selection were that Ma'a Nonu and Mils Muliaina found themselves in the mid-field, Chris Jack and Ali Williams filled the second row, and the Fijians Rokocoko and Sivivatu were paired up on the wings.

Not surprisingly, the French *were* much tougher than the week before. In a tighter match, the difference between the two generals at first-five was a feature, Dan Carter proving he was world-class while Damien Traille showed how lucky he was to be playing pivot in a team renowned for some very classy backs over the years.

Henry showed a willingness to clear the bench in the second half but it was surprising that in a match the All Blacks seemed to have in control, he wasn't prepared to give Nick Evans more than seven minutes at first-five, late in the match. All Black supporters still asked themselves the unbearable question, 'What if Carter is injured?' Evans was now viewed as the number-one back-up to Carter, and it remained a valid criticism of Henry that he was prepared to rotate players in all other positions — but was he doing enough to develop back-ups for his two superstars, Carter and McCaw?

For the record, Carter's 13-point tally established an All Black record of 170 points for the calendar year, passing the 1999 tally of 166 set by Andrew Mehrtens.

WIN	LOSS		
33	**4**	Date	25 November 2006
		Venue	Cardiff
		Against	Wales
		Score	45 – 10

Significant factors

The predominant feature of this match came before the game had even started — there was no haka performed on the field prior to the match, due to a dispute between the All Blacks and Welsh Rugby Union management. Instead it was performed in the dressing room and replayed on the stadium screen once the match had started. The controversy appeared to fire up Henry's men for a match in which they might otherwise have struggled to motivate themselves.

Wales coach Gareth Jenkins summed up the All Blacks' complete dominance when he said, post-match, 'They are the best side in the world, they proved it today. They played some great rugby, their efficiency in the contact area was superb, and when they got the ball their ability to move it wide was superb. We have got to be honest with ourselves and raise our standards.'

Up 28 – 3 at halftime, once again it seemed that Henry missed a prime opportunity to give Nick Evans at least half a match on tour. He finally came on for the last quarter and straightaway broke the line with his first touch, to put Sivivatu in for the last of his hat-trick of tries.

It's very hard to be *too* critical of Henry. The end-of-year tour had confirmed he was on-track in his attempt to nurture two players in each position by the time the World Cup came round. Captain Richie McCaw confirmed he felt things were going the right way: 'I think we have taken a step up. We are happy with what we achieved in terms of how we played . . . We had thirty-two players on this tour who have all contributed.'

The Conditioning
Period

When Henry first came up with the conditioning
concept it was incorrectly interpreted by many people
to be a holiday for twenty-two players. The sacrifice
was massive for New Zealand rugby. Its success could
only be judged at the end of the World Cup.

- Was conditioning too much of a gamble?

- If the theory was correct, why did so many players
  show such poor form when they returned to
  rugby?

- How much did conditioning cost some players?

GRAHAM HENRY'S DECISION to rest twenty-two players for the first half of the Super 14 competition was undoubtedly the most significant and controversial move he made in his campaign towards the 2007 World Cup. Along with his rotation of players in test matches, it was also the most gutsy move Henry had made in his coaching career.

The twenty-two players were named on 11 September 2006, before the conclusion of the Air New Zealand Cup and prior to the end-of-year tour of Europe. This was to give the Super 14 franchises time to plan their campaigns and identify players who would join their squads while these twenty-two All Blacks weren't available.

THE CONDITIONED TWENTY-TWO

Forwards	Backs
Jerry Collins (Wellington)	Dan Carter (Canterbury)
Jason Eaton (Taranaki)	Byron Kelleher (Waikato)
Carl Hayman (Otago)	Leon MacDonald (Canterbury)
Andrew Hore (Taranaki)	Aaron Mauger (Canterbury)
Chris Jack (Tasman)	Mils Muliaina (Waikato)
Richie McCaw (Canterbury)	Joe Rokocoko (Auckland)
Chris Masoe (Wellington)	Sitiveni Sivivatu (Waikato)
Keven Mealamu (Auckland)	Piri Weepu (Wellington)
Anton Oliver (Otago)	
Greg Somerville (Canterbury)	
Rodney So'oialo (Wellington)	
Reuben Thorne (Canterbury)	
Ali Williams (Auckland)	
Tony Woodcock (North Harbour)	

Soon after the announcement of the protected players, Henry explained some of the theory behind his decision to embark on such a dramatic scheme. 'Many of our best athletes have played several years of continuous rugby without a chance to really get their bodies right,' he said. 'The conditioning programme is important for their wellbeing in the long term and also important to our chances of winning the World Cup.' Henry made it clear that being in this select group of twenty-two didn't automatically mean players would be in the World Cup squad. 'We have included twenty-two of our leading players in the conditioning programme, but there are no guarantees. There is a long way to go before we name the World Cup squad and a large group of players are pushing for selection. The door is definitely open.'

'We have included twenty-two of our leading players in the conditioning programme, but there are no guarantees.' — Graham Henry

---

While Henry may have believed this at the time, it was a point that was disputed by many rugby followers once the players returned from their conditioning. Wynne Gray, the leading rugby writer with the *New Zealand Herald*, summed up their feelings at the end of the Super 14 competition when he wrote:

> No matter which way Henry tries to cut it, the conditioned squad were assured selection in the shadow World Cup squad when they were picked last October [sic] — that gave them a false sense of security.

The idea that the emphasis was on the long-term goal of the World Cup would be one Henry continually harped back to during the next twelve months. It was a concept people either found hard to accept or didn't want to accept. They didn't want to have to wait until late October to find out if conditioning had been successful; they wanted to know straightaway.

The man in charge of overseeing the conditioning period, All Black trainer Graham Lowe, shed some light on the conditioning period when interviewed towards the end of the Super 14. Here are his thoughts on aspects of the controversial programme.

Why did the conditioning period take place?
It was an opportunity to give these guys a chance to have a preseason. They do it in other sports internationally, like rugby league, American football and soccer, but our guys who go on the end-of-year tours and have the other campaigns during the year don't get a chance to get their preparation right. What we targeted was an opportunity for these players to prepare themselves adequately for the big year ahead.

What was worked on during the conditioning period?
We looked at the players' strengths and weaknesses, and mainly focused on the areas of their game that they could work on. We looked at key areas such as strength, power and speed. Within this there are obviously different demands from position to position, such as from our props to our locks. The programme was really made up of work in the gym combined with field-based work in the form of running, speed work, while also mixing in things like boxing and wrestling. It was also important that we incorporated an opportunity for the players to transition from this programme back onto the rugby field.

What were some of the individual differences within the conditioning?
Looking at a couple of forwards, someone like Carl Hayman has training experience while Jason Eaton is newer to the scene. We had a strong focus on power and strength gains and muscle-mass gains with Eaton. That was definitely a factor with Hayman, but was not as important.

What did players gain from conditioning?
We've had some very positive results in terms of our speed. Some of the performance gains that we received were from between .05 to .1 of a second over 20 to 30 metres. Some people had significant gains. Joe Rocokoco, Dan Carter, Anton Oliver and Leon MacDonald are some names that spring to mind.

Would conditioning help with injury prevention?
Absolutely. There are some injuries that are just part of the game, like Conrad Smith's broken leg last year. Then there are the other injuries like calf injuries and hamstring strains. To an extent Jerry Collins' shoulder injury was an example of this, with the repetitive damage he had to his shoulder. The programme gave us a chance to address these injury problems. We call it rehab, and in some cases we call it prehab. We're trying to reduce their chances of getting injured as well as dealing with any injuries they've got. When they're getting battered each week and getting new niggles, it is very tough to make changes within a player. Having a concentrated window like this really gave us a chance to clear things up with the goal of keeping the player in a position for the year when they've made significant gains mentally and physically.

Did players largely stay clear of contact during this period?
Yes, definitely. What we were after here was to avoid the potential niggles associated with contact so they didn't interfere with our ability to consolidate the other variables

they had. Our programme involved three blocks. At the end of each one we'd reassess the players. As we came into the third block, on the back of that we put a transition, which was really the idea that we needed to bring them from training that doesn't involve contact back towards the specific demands of playing rugby in their positions. We really thought this would help us to consolidate and establish the gains the players had made. And our obvious goal was to carry those through to the World Cup.

What about specific requirements, such as skill work?
It was definitely part of it. We talked about the idea that there was a 'needs' window, not just a conditioning window, because we had to acknowledge that there was a mental and physical component to what these players were doing. For example, players had an opportunity during conditioning to have a weekend for themselves. From a skill-development perspective, the coaches worked hard with the players around that and it was integrated into the programme. We also dealt with their leadership and mental development. We wanted to make sure we covered all the components we could address in a positive way during this period without overloading the players.

How closely were the twenty-two players monitored?
We worked really hard with the franchises in the programme development. I spent a lot of time travelling last year, ensuring we had good set-ups within the franchises. We get regular feedback from the people delivering the programmes. The players themselves also had a facility for providing feedback via the internet. Obviously we had fitness testing done on a regular basis. All the strength and power monitoring stuff got collected, so we knew how they were coping in the gym. We didn't want to be Big Brother with it, but we wanted to make sure that as they responded to the programme we were able to react and get the best for each player.

What were management's expectations for the period?

We spent a lot of time as a management group. I think the key factor I hope people could take away from this is that it wasn't an invention that was plucked out of the blue. It was absolutely the concept of a pre-season for these players — so they got the opportunity to get the pre-season that most players strive for and don't often get. For example, from 2006 the players would only have had two, maybe three, weeks of solid conditioning to prepare them for a whole season of rugby before they were back into playing pre-season matches again. We always thought we'd get great results, and hopefully that is what showed through in the way players performed when they came back to the playing field.

It was the million-dollar question — would conditioning work? Getting no clear-cut answer didn't help rugby followers with their reaction. They wanted an immediate answer — but of course the real answer wouldn't come till the business end of the World Cup.

The major thing in Henry's favour was his freedom to argue that nothing had worked for New Zealand coaches since the All Blacks won the inaugural World Cup in 1987, so people who didn't have a clue what conditioning was about were prepared to accept 'different will be better'.

When it came to the specifics of who should be in the conditioning group, it was never viewed as strictly the top twenty-two players. For instance, a player like Keith Robinson might have been seen as one of the best locks at the time by the selectors, but it was obvious after his injury problems during 2006 that he was in need of playing time. In contrast, it was just as obvious that a player like Jason Eaton needed a considerable amount of bulk added to his frame, and would benefit from gym work during a conditioning period much more than Robinson.

The most controversial aspect of the All Blacks' conditioning was the impact it was always going to have on the Super 14 competition. Undoubtedly all the New Zealand teams would be considerably under-strength for the first half of the competition, therefore affecting not only the New Zealand teams' results but also the overall quality of the competition.

In Henry's defence, Australia and South Africa were both still struggling to come to grips with the extra team they'd acquired when the competition had been expanded in 2006 from its previous format of twelve teams. Resting a large group of their players would have been catastrophic for their teams, yet with New Zealand's superior player depth we were still able to get the Blues and the Crusaders into the semi-finals of the Super 14. The support of senior officials in the NZRU was always going to be necessary for Henry to go ahead with such an innovative move, and to his relief they were united in their support of him. Both Australia and South Africa considered their own ways of resting players, but their lack of depth meant it was impractical for them to follow New Zealand's lead.

> **With New Zealand's superior player depth we were still able to get the Blues and the Crusaders into the semi-finals of the Super 14.**

However, halfway through the Tri-Nations South African coach Jake White decided to rest more than twenty of his top players from the Australasian leg of the tournament. This decision came after a large number of his players had picked up injuries and were showing signs of fatigue.

The CEO of the Australian Rugby Union, John O'Neill, expressed strong opposition to the South African move. O'Neill was so scathing of what White did that it leaves little doubt New Zealand would never have been able to rest their players during the Super 14 if O'Neill had been in power nine months earlier. He was most infuriated by White's suggestion that a broken rib to Bobby Skinstad, incurred in South Africa's loss to Australia, justified his decision to rest leading players like Victor Matfield, Schalk Burger and Bryan Habana. O'Neill's reply made it very clear where he stood on the issue of resting players for the sake of the World Cup. 'Some of the stuff Jake White has said are the most extraordinary of contradictions,' he said. 'He is basically saying that because Bobby Skinstad has a broken rib, that supports his decision to leave all the players behind. He is basically saying that his only objective this year is the World Cup. He has made it clear that whatever he has to do in between — so be it.'

Needless to say, O'Neill's view on the All Blacks' conditioning programme would have made for some priceless entertainment had he been in rugby at the time.

Prior to the team's match against the All Blacks at Christchurch, White acknowledged his timing wasn't ideal but also explained that, unlike Graham Henry, he'd had little choice. 'South African rugby does not have as much depth as a country like New Zealand. We had twelve injuries last year to top-line players, and that clearly influenced my thinking,' he explained. 'But also, our franchises in South Africa kept their players going through the whole Super 14, unlike New Zealand's model. Also, there was the continual pressure of the sports scientists back home saying to me, you need to rest the top guys. If that means maybe I disappointed the public because they expected the big names to be here, I apologize for that. If we didn't give them enough notice to avoid buying tickets they might not have done, I am sorry. There was no intention whatsoever to deceive people.'

There was a long-term positive spin-off for New Zealand rugby from resting current All Blacks, in that giving more players match time helped widen New Zealand's talent base even further. A prime example of this was the promising first five-eighth Stephen Brett getting consistent game time with the Crusaders when Dan Carter's presence would otherwise have ensured that he warmed the bench.

While there was no O'Neill around to prevent the conditioning from taking place, there was still some strong opposition to it from out of Australia. One person who was highly critical was New South Wales coach Ewen McKenzie. On 12 January McKenzie said, 'I am disappointed. The brand is the total brand and we all have our responsibilities looking after that . . . We all contribute to the brand and I think that [the playing ban] does have an impact on the brand. It does change the competition, it doesn't matter what you say . . . By the time you get to the end of the competition some teams are going to have had a theoretically easier run. They are going to score artificial points and be in a different place than they normally would be. They [the conditioned players] will do the preparation off the field and eventually they will get on the field to play. But in that period, it will be interesting to see if they don't get any injuries. They will have been out for a significant period, and contact-fit is like with a boxer: taking hits in a game is different than in training.'

A number of injuries to the twenty-two protected players soon after their return to Super 14 rugby would suggest McKenzie is right, and casts doubt on Graham Lowe's assertion that the conditioning period would help with injury prevention. Mils Muliaina, Sitiveni Sivivatu, Byron Kelleher, Joe Rokocoko, Jerry Collins, Jason Eaton, Chris Jack and Daniel Carter all suffered injuries in the early stages of their return to rugby.

When you combined this problem with the three Auckland players struggling to get back into their team, Henry must have had doubts about the value of the conditioning programme. Over half of his players had not only missed the first half of the Super 14 competition, but had also missed much of the second half as well.

Former Wallaby captain Mark Loane was another Australian highly critical of the conditioning period. On 14 February Loane said, 'They are doing a peculiar thing of trying to protect their players from playing too much rugby; it's a very, very strange thing. If you are going to be a very good bricklayer, you need to lay bricks; if you're going to be a good carpenter, you have to drive a few nails into pieces of wood. It's a peculiar thing to me; they are going to try and make their rugby players better by not allowing them to play rugby at certain times, so I think it might be very, very difficult for New Zealand because of the internal expectations.'

A number of injuries to the twenty-two protected players soon after their return to Super 14 rugby casts doubt on Graham Lowe's assertion that the conditioning period would help with injury prevention.

Henry had the support of many well-informed people back in New Zealand though, one of whom was former All Blacks trainer Jim Blair. On 26 February Blair said, 'The whole point of being fit is so that you can forget about it when you are playing. You don't want to be saying to yourself, I won't run over there because I might not make it back again. These guys will take enormous confidence out of being stronger and being able to run faster for longer. The other good thing about the conditioning group is that it will provide that little bit of a prod for the rest of the group. Apart from one or two guys, no one is certain of being picked, and professional teams need that element of competition. Everyone will be looking over their shoulder and teams need that wee bit of fear. I think it will be a real eye-opener when these guys come back and play.'

In my opinion, Henry's commitment to the conditioning programme became almost obsessive. He was intolerant of those questioning it, even when those questions were reasonable and balanced. As it turned out, Jim Blair's claim that 'it will be a real eye-opener when these guys come back and play' could not have been more wrong. Most of the players performed below their normal standards, and the rugby public had never seen stars like McCaw and Carter play so poorly.

Conditioning — or *reconditioning* as many put it — became one of the most over-used terms in New Zealand sport during the year leading up to the 2007 World Cup, yet few people understood the concept. Once the injury count mounted and players took time to find form, the public and media both became sceptical about conditioning. On one hand, people were prepared to wait for players to peak at the World Cup, but they wanted to see some type of immediate indication that Henry had been barking up the right tree with conditioning.

When no New Zealand team made the final of the Super 14 competition, the knives were out for Henry.

It didn't help that there was a misunderstanding as to what Henry intended to achieve from the conditioning period. Many people interpreted it as an extended holiday for players, as opposed to an opportunity to give them time to build up a base of fitness, strength and power that many of them hadn't been able to do before. There was also concern as to how individual teams would perform without their stars, and about the quality of the Super 14 competition as a whole. When no New Zealand team made the final of the competition, the knives were out for Henry.

Jim Kayes, writing in the *Dominion* on 14 May, summed up what many people felt at the time.

Only a skilled politician could argue that the World Cup conditioning programme has been anything but damaging to the Super 14 in New Zealand.

Poor play, small crowds and reduced television audiences robbed the competition of its lustre, and the conditioning programme also hobbled the Hurricanes, Crusaders and Blues, and opened the door to a South African revival.

The form of the Bulls and Sharks will not automatically translate into success for the Springboks at the World Cup in France, but it will help.

Henry stuck to his guns and grabbed the opportunity to reinforce to people that his conditioning window was more about the long term. The *New Zealand Herald* reported on 14 May that Henry said:

We are hoping guys will peak in August–September. They are not expected to peak in May, so that was the reason for the conditioning window — so that these guys haven't played thirty-odd games during that calendar year and if they had done that, they would have fallen over. So hopefully, they will peak at the right time of the year, which is obviously September–October.

Most of Henry's select group of twenty-two players struggled with their re-entry to the Super 14, and this was especially noticeable in the early weeks of their return to the playing field. The biggest hiccup came within the Blues franchise, where coach David Nucifora preferred to leave many players who had been performing well for him in their positions rather than introduce players he knew would be down on match fitness.

This created difficulties for two players in particular: Ali Williams and Joe Rokocoko. Joe barely got a chance to get any form and prove himself, whereas Ali's frustrations at being continually benched culminated in him getting sent home from South Africa by the Blues. All Black hooker Keven Mealamu also had a frustrating period round this time as Derren Witcombe was often preferred, despite many critics rating Mealamu the best rake in the world.

On the other hand, three players in the Blues benefited from regular and consistent game time. Isaia Toeava was one of the standout players, and this ensured that come test time he was given the opportunity to prove his worth at centre for the All Blacks.

Doug Howlett looked fresh and keen, and back to some of the best form of his career. Admittedly he was aided by the fact that he hadn't gone on the end-of-year tour, so he'd given his body a good rest. Breaking the Super 14 try-scoring record didn't do him any harm, reminding the All Black selectors of his worth. His form was rewarded when the international season began and it became clear he had leap-frogged Rico Gear in the pecking order for an All Black wing position.

> **The absence of the conditioned All Blacks in the early rounds of the Super 14 and their poor form when they joined the competition unquestionably gave South Africa momentum in World Cup year.**

Troy Flavell was the third person who relished the extra games. His absence from the conditioning group enabled him to captain the Blues, and the additional responsibility appeared to benefit his play. However, it could be argued that his heavy workload led to a loss of form towards the end of the Super 14 and his subsequent dropping from the All Black squad.

The absence of the conditioned All Blacks in the early rounds of the Super 14 and their poor form when they joined the competition unquestionably gave South Africa momentum in World Cup year. While New Zealand rugby fans were harping on about incompetent Australian referees, weakened New Zealand franchise teams and the poor form of their stars, South African rugby was once again on a roll. Springbok fans were no longer worried about quotas and politics, but were focused on the Bulls and the Sharks. A new confidence had been born in the republic, and only time would tell whether it would again become a crescendo of arrogance reminiscent of the glory days of Springbok rugby.

Would the defeat at Rustenburg, along with conditioning, provide the basis for a South African renaissance that would come back and bite Henry on the backside at the World Cup? Only time would tell.

The Build-up — World Cup Year

The matches against France C, Canada and South Africa B were the worst possible preparation for the All Blacks' quest to win the World Cup. Test-match status was degraded and the quality of the rugby was poor. People began to question whether these sacrifices were worth it for the sake of the World Cup.

- Had there been any progress with the centre position?

- Did back-ups for Carter or McCaw get enough game time?

- Did weak opposition during 2007 affect the All Blacks' performances at the World Cup?

ON 20 MAY 2007, Graham Henry announced his first All Black squad for the tests against France and Canada and the Tri-Nations. It was significant, as it revealed the base of players Henry envisaged taking through to the World Cup in France. It is now interesting to look back and see that twenty-seven of the thirty-man squad went on to be named on 22 July as his final World Cup squad.

The thirty-man squad announced in May 2007 was:

Dan Carter, Jerry Collins, Nick Evans,
Troy Flavell, Carl Hayman, Andrew Hore,
Doug Howlett, Chris Jack, Byron Kelleher,
Brendon Leonard, Luke McAlister,
Richie McCaw (capt), Leon MacDonald,
Chris Masoe, Aaron Mauger,
Keven Mealamu, Mils Muliaina,
Anton Oliver, Keith Robinson,
Joe Rokocoko, John Schwalger,
Sitiveni Sivivatu, Conrad Smith,
Rodney So'oialo, Reuben Thorne,
Neemia Tialata, Isaia Toeava, Piri Weepu,
Ali Williams, Tony Woodcock.

The squad was largely predictable, except for two new caps, Waikato halfback Brendon Leonard and Wellington prop John Schwalger, with Leonard in particular showing brilliant Super 14 form to jump ahead of people like Jimmy Cowan and Andy Ellis. Meanwhile, Schwalger was being seen as the man to do Greg Somerville's job, covering both sides of the scrum while the veteran Canterbury prop recovered from an operation to repair his Achilles tendon. Rico Gear and Ma'a Nonu were viewed as two of the more unlucky players to miss selection for the squad. Those unavailable for selection due to injury were James Ryan, Jason Eaton, Greg Somerville and Sione Lauaki, who had undergone surgery on both knees the week before the squad was named.

FOR THE RECORD

Here's how it played out on the field.

WIN	LOSS		
1	**—**	Date	**2 June 2007**
		Venue	**Auckland**
		Against	**France**
		Score	**42 – 11**

The team named to play

Leon MacDonald, Joe Rokocoko, Isaia Toeava, Aaron Mauger, Sitiveni Sivivatu, Daniel Carter, Piri Weepu, Chris Masoe, Richie McCaw (capt), Reuben Thorne, Ali Williams, Chris Jack, Carl Hayman, Keven Mealamu, Tony Woodcock.

Reserves: Andrew Hore, Neemia Tialata, Troy Flavell, Rodney So'oialo, Brendon Leonard, Nick Evans, Ma'a Nonu.

Significant factors

Injuries meant five players were unavailable for selection for the All Blacks' first test of the year. Mils Muliaina, Conrad Smith and Byron Kelleher all had hamstring strains, while flanker Jerry Collins' heel and Anton Oliver's foot kept them out.

Henry opted for a conservative team, and his loyalty to players who had done the job for him so far with the All Blacks continued to show in many selections. In particular, Reuben Thorne, Leon MacDonald and Joe Rokocoko were selections based much more on what they'd done for him in the past than on Super 14 form. Ma'a Nonu's spot on the bench could be viewed the same way, after he'd been called into the squad to cover injuries. He had been struggling with injury himself the previous week, while in camp with the Junior All Blacks.

Ali Williams' return to the playing field was widely expected, as it was common knowledge that Henry knew how to get the best out of him. The most interesting experiment proved to be using Masoe to start the match at number 8, leaving So'oialo on the bench.

The French had selected an under-strength squad to tour, with most of their top players unavailable because of club commitments — an indictment on the IRB and the decision-makers. By the time the first test came around the French had been nicknamed 'France C' by the New Zealand media. The team they ended up with for the first test contained eleven debutants, so they were always going to be up against it.

Playing their first match of the year, the home side were not at their best and displayed signs of rustiness, squandering a series of scoring opportunities through sloppy handling. However, they were still able to pile on the points against a team whose sole resemblance to the European champions was the blue jersey. In particular, there was too much lateral ball movement without first doing the hard yards. In the past, consistent go-forward had often been a problem in Henry's sides when Jerry Collins wasn't playing, and again it was clear how much his contribution was missed.

Playing their first match of the year, the home side were not at their best and displayed signs of rustiness.

Up front it was encouraging to see a strong return to international rugby by Ali Williams, especially after the frustrations he and the All Black coaching staff had endured during the Super 14 while he was benched by the Blues.

Aaron Mauger and Sitiveni Sivivatu scored two tries apiece, while replacement forward Rodney So'oialo touched down in the second half after captain Richie McCaw and fly-half Dan Carter were taken off with minor injuries at the interval.

Reuben Thorne took over as captain for the second half while So'oialo went to number 8 and Masoe shuffled to openside. Carter's ankle injury enabled Nick Evans to get a full half of rugby at first-five, and he seemed to relish playing with good players around him again after his Highlanders team had been so reliant on him to create things for them in the Super 14. Brendon Leonard combined well with Evans and had a very promising debut.

WIN	LOSS		
2	**–**	Date	**9 June 2007**
		Venue	**Wellington**
		Against	**France**
		Score	**61 – 10**

The team named to play

Leon MacDonald, Joe Rokocoko, Isaia Toeava, Luke McAlister, Sitiveni Sivivatu, Nick Evans, Byron Kelleher, Rodney So'oialo, Richie McCaw (capt), Jerry Collins, Ali Williams, Chris Jack, Carl Hayman, Anton Oliver, Tony Woodcock.

Reserves: Keven Mealamu, Neemia Tialata, Troy Flavell, Chris Masoe, Brendon Leonard, Ma'a Nonu, Doug Howlett.

Significant factors

Just as in the first test of the year, Henry's selection was again largely dictated by injuries. In particular a calf injury to Keith Robinson, as he was warming up to start the match, meant Troy Flavell came onto the bench and Chris Jack shuffled off it and into the starting line-up.

Dan Carter was the major omission from the match, though it was a blessing in disguise for Henry, able to give Nick Evans more time to try to cement his place as the second-choice first-five.

Conrad Smith was supposed to be on the bench but had re-injured his hamstring mid-week at training. When Aaron Mauger was also injured during training, Ma'a Nonu was brought back into the squad. Doug Howlett was the other player added to the twenty-two with all the reshuffling.

The win was generally regarded as much more convincing than

the previous week; however, the standout moment of the match was a negative for the All Blacks. Ali Williams broke his jaw tackling French hardman Sebastien Chabal, forcing Troy Flavell to play fifty-one minutes of the match even though he hadn't even been in the playing squad when he arrived at the ground.

Joe Rokocoko's two tries also had people shaking their heads at his lack of Super 14 game time with the Blues, and question marks remained about whether Toeava could fill the vital centre position at international level. The hot-and-cold nature of his play was acutely obvious when he scored a great individual try in the second half only to drop a sitter of a pass less than two minutes later. Leonard had more than thirty minutes' game time and made sure he was pencilled in by the selectors as the third halfback to take to the World Cup.

At first-five Evans turned in a solid performance, reaffirming his status as Carter's understudy. However, Luke McAlister was preferred as goalkicker, when it would have seemed logical to give Evans a chance to prove he could replace Carter as both a player and goalkicker if necessary. As it turned out, McAlister kicked poorly, missing five of his twelve attempts at goal — a concern, considering there was no pressure on him.

WIN	LOSS		
3	–	Date	16 June 2007
		Venue	Hamilton
		Against	Canada
		Score	64 – 13

The team named to play

Mils Muliaina, Doug Howlett, Luke McAlister, Aaron Mauger, Sitiveni Sivivatu, Daniel Carter, Byron Kelleher, Jerry Collins, Chris Masoe, Reuben Thorne (capt), Ross Filipo, Troy Flavell, Neemia Tialata, Andrew Hore, John Schwalger.

Reserves: Keven Mealamu, Carl Hayman, Rodney So'oialo, Richie McCaw, Piri Weepu, Rico Gear, Leon MacDonald.

Significant factors

Reuben Thorne starting as captain was the feature selection, along with Chris Masoe as openside flanker. Injuries to Ali Williams, Keith Robinson and Greg Rawlinson, together with Chris Jack on paternity leave, meant that Troy Flavell and test debutant Ross Filipo were selected at lock. An all-Hurricanes front row was rotated in, while Luke McAlister on trial at centre showed that Henry was beginning to clutch at straws in his search for the best number 13 available.

The All Blacks were better — but not even close to hitting their straps. They lacked continuity throughout the team, particularly in the backline.

Credit should be given to the Canadians for providing stiffer opposition in this test than most people expected. Their commitment was good and their defence well organized. The All Blacks were better — but not even close to hitting their straps. They lacked continuity throughout the team, particularly in the backline. A particularly scathing critic was former All Black Josh Kronfeld, who wrote in his weekly column in the *Sunday News*:

> There is nothing happening on the All Blacks' attack. Nothing . . . The team are devoid of any quality moves to try and create holes in the opposition. There are too many people standing off waiting to be put into space instead of playing to a pattern to try and create that space. I've heard the argument that Graham Henry has instructed the side to keep their attacking game plan away from World Cup spies, but that doesn't wash with me.

The experiments with McAlister and Masoe didn't provide the answers for centre or for back-up openside flanker for Richie McCaw. Indications were also there that McAlister wasn't suited to the number 13 jersey, while Masoe continued his average 2007 form on the openside flank. In the makeshift second row, Troy Flavell and debutant Ross Filipo held their own against the big men in the Canadian pack.

Dan Carter still didn't look anywhere near his best form following injuries and the conditioning period. Despite scoring three tries, he was critical of his own game post-match. 'It has been frustrating. I haven't had three games together in a row, which hasn't been ideal. I still see I've got a long way to go yet. I wasn't pleased with that performance,' he said.

WIN 4	LOSS –	Date	23 June 2007
		Venue	Durban
		Against	South Africa
		Score	26 – 21

The team named to play
Mils Muliaina, Joe Rokocoko, Isaia Toeava, Aaron Mauger, Sitiveni Sivivatu, Daniel Carter, Byron Kelleher, Rodney So'oialo, Richie McCaw (capt), Jerry Collins, Greg Rawlinson, Troy Flavell, Carl Hayman, Anton Oliver, Tony Woodcock.

Reserves: Keven Mealamu, Neemia Tialata, Ross Filipo, Chris Masoe, Piri Weepu, Luke McAlister, Leon MacDonald.

Significant factors
This was the first real test of 2007 for Henry's men. For New Zealand rugby supporters the anticipation of a contest where the outcome wasn't known prior to kick-off meant the match was eagerly awaited.

The test was just as important for Jake White. After his team's late rally to beat Australia the previous week, White was caught on video telling his team just how much all matches against New Zealand meant. 'It was unbelievable [against Australia], but I never doubted you,' said White. 'You've got the All Blacks next week. Now it gets even harder, but we get born to play rugby against New Zealand. That's why we get born in this country.'

The public front Graham Henry put up going into the match was somewhat different. He came out with the statement that rugby is 'just a game' as he justified Chris Jack's decision to stay at home on paternity leave rather than travel to South Africa.

The South African team named for the match was significantly under-strength due to injuries. The unavailability of Bryan Habana, Fourie du Preez, Andre Pretorius, Pierre Spies, Juan Smith, Gurthro Steenkamp and regular skipper John Smit meant the Springboks were without nearly half of their top starting line-up. In contrast, lock was the only area in which the All Blacks were under-strength. Jack's absence, plus many injuries, meant Rawlinson and Flavell started in the second row, despite both of them coming well down the selection pecking order.

The intensity and vigour both teams brought to the match were outstanding, with the All Blacks forced into many mistakes as a result of South Africa's aggressive tackling and their very flat defence, which as usual verged on being offside. After the match Aaron Mauger expressed disappointment in the South Africans' dirty tactics. 'There was a lot of cheap shots going into the side there,' he said. 'Fair is fair if you are ready for it and shaping up. But a lot of it is coming in from the side of rucks and that sort of stuff. It's pretty average really, so it's something to think about the next time we play them.'

The intensity and vigour both teams brought to the match were outstanding, with the All Blacks forced into many mistakes as a result of South Africa's aggressive tackling and their very flat defence, which as usual verged on being offside.

The first half was a tug-of-war and was tied at 6 – 6 just before the break. A great lineout drive by the South Africans close to the line saw them take the lead 11 – 6 going into the break. Lineouts again remained a concern for the All Blacks, with the South Africans continuing the dominance they had achieved in recent years. An All Black reluctance to challenge for the ball on the South Africans' throws also continued.

Both coaches highlighted the fresher legs of the All Blacks' reserves and conditioned players as a crucial factor in the All Blacks moving ahead in the final quarter of the match. South Africa's fatigue hadn't been helped by Pedro Wannenburg being sin-binned after fifteen minutes of the second half for his team's continual infringing at the breakdown.

The All Black loose-forward trio was outstanding and proved to be one of the most decisive differences between the two teams. A memorable 40-metre run by So'oialo, with only twelve minutes to go in the game, led to Richie McCaw crashing over for the try which brought his team within 2 points of the South Africans.

Finally some luck went the way of the All Blacks, when J.P. Pietersen dropped the ball and the match was sealed with a Rokocoko try.

Captain McCaw's main concern looking ahead was that the All Blacks needed to start stronger. 'The key is to get it going from the start because some days you don't get out of jail,' he said. 'It'll be great to be able to start the way we finished.'

WIN	LOSS		
4	**1**	Date	30 June 2007
		Venue	Melbourne
		Against	Australia
		Score	15 – 20

The team named to play

Mils Muliaina, Rico Gear, Luke McAlister, Aaron Mauger, Joe Rokocoko, Dan Carter, Byron Kelleher, Rodney So'oialo, Richie

McCaw (capt), Jerry Collins, Troy Flavell, Chris Jack, Carl Hayman, Anton Oliver, Tony Woodcock.

Reserves: Keven Mealamu, Neemia Tialata, Ross Filipo, Chris Masoe, Piri Weepu, Sitiveni Sivivatu, Nick Evans.

Significant factors

In light of South Africa's announcement early in the week that they'd be resting twenty of their top players for their final two matches of the Tri-Nations, Graham Henry made this statement on announcing his team to take on Australia: 'The Bledisloe Cup means a lot to the team and to New Zealanders, and we have selected our best team. It's not the same team as last week, but it's our best.'

Was it really Henry's 'best' team? The major change from the South African clash came at centre, with Isaia Toeava's shoulder injury leaving him unavailable for selection. With Conrad Smith still recovering from his hamstring injury, once again the All Black centre position became the main topic of pre-match debate. Initially Henry named a backline with Luke McAlister at second-five, Mils Muliaina at centre and MacDonald at fullback.

After Mauger's top-notch performance the previous week, many people debated whether McAlister could genuinely be viewed as the 'best available' second-five. As things turned out, a groin injury to MacDonald on the Thursday leading up to the match meant a reshuffle of the backline, Mauger starting at second-five with McAlister outside him. Mils Muliaina returned to his favoured fullback spot. Many also debated whether Anton Oliver really was the best hooker to start this match, ahead of Keven Mealamu. The fact that Sivivatu was initially rested but then called up to the bench at the last minute, following Mauger's injury, confirmed an element of Graham Henry telling people what he thought they wanted to hear.

It couldn't have been a better start for the All Blacks, and they were up 7 – 0 after three minutes when Tony Woodcock crashed over for a well-taken try. Their ball-handling let them down in the first half, yet when Rico Gear went over in the 25th minute they still found themselves with a comfortable 15 – 6 lead. They could have all but wrapped up the match in the 34th minute of the first half, but Rodney So'oialo dropped a pass that would almost certainly have seen the All Blacks at 22 – 6 with halftime approaching.

One ominous sign was Dan Carter continuing to look well off his best. In particular he put the ball out on the full twice in the first half, and his goalkicking was also poor.

Henry made a significant call, replacing three players just six minutes into the second half. These were obviously pre-planned substitutions and no indication of the way the players coming off had performed. Oliver, Woodcock and Flavell were replaced by Mealamu, Tialata and Filipo; Oliver and Woodcock in particular had done everything asked of them. The substitution of Kelleher four minutes later also seemed pre-planned.

The sin-binning of Carl Hayman in the 60th minute was a crucial turning point in the match, and a highly debatable decision by referee Marius Jonker. However, the All Blacks were their own worst enemy leading up to this decision, showing a marked lack of discipline, and giving away soft penalties. Hayman's yellow card gave the Australians the opening they needed, and two minutes later it was 15 – 13 after they scored and converted a try.

The fact that Rico Gear, Richie McCaw and Chris Jack all had good chances to tackle Adam Ashley-Cooper as he powered in was the most concerning aspect. If defence is as much about mental attitude as many people lead us to believe, where were the heads of these players — especially that of the All Black captain, who had probably never missed such a crucial tackle before?

A great 40-metre run by Stirling Mortlock ten minutes later set Scott Staniforth up for the match-winning try under the posts.

A confusing substitution by Henry came with six minutes to go. The All Blacks' number-one winger, Sitiveni Sivivatu, had initially been left out for this match, with one report saying he had a broken nose. Yet he came on to replace Rokocoko in chilly conditions in Melbourne with the match nearly over — with barely enough time to work up a sweat, let alone impact on the match.

This incident typified the confused mental approach plaguing the All Black build-up to the World Cup at this stage. How much do you wrap your players in cotton wool and how important are winning test matches and building combinations to your progress? Whether Graham Henry had the formula right was now becoming the subject of debate.

For many traditional All Black supporters another point of concern came post-match. To see an All Black coach appearing so unfazed by his team's loss to an average Australian team spoke volumes about where All Black and world rugby was at. To Henry it appeared to be a minor speed bump. He could lose to the South Africans the following week for all he cared, so long as he felt he was on track for the Cup. All his chickens were so obviously in the one basket.

In hindsight it was lucky for Henry that he had conned people into believing his best possible side had taken the field. Those who'd dared to question the All Black rotation system had often been shot down by fans who claimed Henry didn't have any obligation to play his top side, because his teams had been winning anyway. This defeat of an All Black team Henry claimed as his best side by a second-rate Australian team raised real concerns about whether the All Blacks were on the right track. If the chopping and changing continued, could the same thing happen in a vital World Cup game?

WIN	LOSS		
5	1	Date	14 July 2007
		Venue	Christchurch
		Against	South Africa
		Score	33 – 6

The team named to play

Mils Muliaina, Doug Howlett, Isaia Toeava, Luke McAlister, Sitiveni

Sivivatu, Daniel Carter, Piri Weepu, Rodney So'oialo, Richie McCaw (capt), Reuben Thorne, Chris Jack, Keith Robinson, Carl Hayman, Keven Mealamu, Tony Woodcock.

Reserves: Andrew Hore, Neemia Tialata, Jerry Collins, Chris Masoe, Brendon Leonard, Conrad Smith, Nick Evans.

Significant factors

It was no real surprise to see the All Black selectors experiment with their starting team again in the lead-up to this match, given that they lined up against such a weak South African side. Leaving Jerry Collins on the bench was the most confusing selection, considering his well-known love of playing rugby. There also seemed very little need for anyone to learn more about his replacement Reuben Thorne's predictable style of play.

The changes from the Australian test were made mainly to give those who hadn't played much rugby for some time a run. The most confusing selection in the backs was Conrad Smith being left on the bench, when he'd played so little rugby and was clearly viewed by the selectors as one of the top two specialist centres. If he was fit enough to be a reserve, surely he was fit enough to start? Keith Robinson was put straight into the second row.

Despite the South Africans taking the field even more under-strength than against Australia the previous week, they once again turned in a respectable performance, highlighted by a very committed defensive effort.

The All Blacks' performance was plagued with similarities to their losing match against Australia a fortnight earlier. The failure to accurately finish off promising movements was the most frustrating aspect of their play, and continued to haunt them. Even though the All Blacks never looked in danger of losing the match, constant errors meant a mere 12 – 6 score in their favour with twelve minutes of the match remaining. Only then were they able to put the finishing touches on movements and ensure the final score showed some of the wide margin that had been expected.

The All Blacks' ability to cut free in the final quarter of the match was aided considerably by the sin-binning of Springbok flanker Pedrie Wannenburg in the 53rd minute. Referee Stu Dickinson could easily have carded a Springbok player earlier, however, so any advantage the All Blacks gained was balanced by the fact that the Springboks had been lucky to keep fifteen players on the field for so long.

Strong contributions off the bench by Brendon Leonard at halfback and Nick Evans at fullback also deserved some of the kudos for the late flurry of points to the All Blacks. Replacements Collins and Mealamu contributed well and would probably have punished the South Africans much more if they'd been allowed to start the game.

The late scoring by the All Blacks narrowly avoided the potentially embarrassing situation for Henry of being genuinely threatened on the scoreboard by what was effectively South Africa's B team.

While the All Black management put on a positive face after the game and Henry came out with 'A lot of progress was made', in reality his team still wasn't playing as well as he would have wanted, just one match out from the World Cup.

Some of the things Henry did were hard for anyone outside his camp to understand. The decision to bring on Conrad Smith for the last three minutes of the match in conditions close to zero degrees made no practical sense. Smith's hamstring had just overcome a lengthy recovery period, and if any warning had been needed of the risk involved in the cold of Jade Stadium it came in the pre-match warm-up when number-one winger Sitiveni Sivivatu injured his calf muscle. This injury meant Joe Rokocoko, outside the original twenty-two, had to come in to start the match. Adding to the irony of the injury was that Sivivatu himself had been given just six confusing minutes on the field towards the end of the Australian test match.

In reality Henry's team still wasn't playing as well as he would have wanted, just one match out from the World Cup.

The All Black problems gave Springbok coach Jake White weaponry after the match to voice his approval of how things were progressing from his perspective. 'I think the All Blacks probably got a hell of a fright in this game', he said. 'I would hope we have sown sufficient doubt in All Black minds before the World Cup. At halftime, I came down in the lift with Graham Henry and I could see the look on his face. It was 6 – 3 and we had missed a penalty to be 6 all. That was one of the best All Black sides they could have put out against us, so they will have doubts in their minds. You only had to listen to the crowd after sixty minutes to know that. They were thinking, this is not the awesome All Black side that they had in the last couple of years.'

It would be hard not to agree with White. It was much more than just the crowd at the game who were getting frustrated with the fact that the All Blacks couldn't put together a convincing forty-minute performance, let alone a full eighty. White also confirmed the match had proved to him that with his top players back, they could give the All Blacks a real run for their money at the World Cup. 'I have no doubt that if we get our best players ready and go through the same things we have done over and over again, there is no reason why we can't match them.'

The unspectacular effort by the All Blacks at Christchurch meant the Tri-Nations and Bledisloe Cup decider at Eden Park the following week shaped up as the last chance for the All Blacks to show some convincing form in a test match before they headed off to the World Cup in France.

WIN	LOSS
6	1

Date **21 July 2007**
Venue **Auckland**
Against **Australia**
Score **26 – 12**

The team named to play

Mils Muliaina, Doug Howlett, Isaia Toeava, Luke McAlister, Joe Rokocoko, Dan Carter, Byron Kelleher, Rodney So'oialo, Richie McCaw (capt), Jerry Collins, Keith Robinson, Chris Jack, Carl Hayman, Anton Oliver, Tony Woodcock.

Reserves: Keven Mealamu, Neemia Tialata, Reuben Thorne, Chris Masoe, Brendon Leonard, Aaron Mauger, Nick Evans.

Significant factors

Ali Williams, Leon MacDonald and Sitiveni Sivivatu all remained injured but apart from them, it genuinely appeared that this time Henry was fronting up with his best available team in a match built up as the perfect dress-rehearsal for the All Blacks going into the World Cup. Not only was there pressure on the All Blacks to win the Tri-Nations and the Bledisloe Cup, but the match also served as a great opportunity to prove to themselves and their fans that they were making progress as a team. In the selections it appeared there wasn't much between McAlister and Mauger at second-five, and some speculated about whether speaking out against the rotation policy the previous week had come back to bite Mauger.

Conrad Smith was deemed 'too risky' to even make the bench, which meant he was likely to receive World Cup selection the day after the Eden Park test despite having played only three and a half minutes of international rugby all year.

Unfortunately, heavy rain meant the All Blacks were never going to be able to express themselves as they might have wanted during this match. What the rain did do, though, was force the All Blacks to control the ball and tidy up a nagging problem from previous matches. They were lucky to hold a 12 – 9 lead at halftime after they lost four lineouts on their own throw. This led to a frustrating half where the Australians dominated possession and territory. Fortunately for the All Blacks, the Wallabies lacked the ability to genuinely threaten them, relying too much on Stirling Mortlock and missing the suspended Lote Tuqiri.

In such a close match, neither teams messed around when bringing key men into the game during the second half. Chris Latham came on only five minutes into the second half for the Australians, and Leonard and Mealamu entered the game for the All Blacks two minutes later. Henry had shown in the previous match that he was keen to bring on fresh legs at hooker and halfback with about half an hour to go. His favourite line during the Tri-Nations had been that 'it is a twenty-two-man game these days' and he seemed intent on proving it. Two substitutions were made early in the second spell. Kelleher had played his worst half as an All Black and Oliver's lack of combination with his jumpers and lifters at lineout time caused huge problems.

> These lessons seemed to be taking a long time to learn — much longer than you'd expect from the top-ranked side in world rugby.

The lineout remained a worry, especially the way forwards coach Steve Hansen brushed off concerns after the match by saying it would have been a problem if they hadn't turned things around in the second half. The reality remained that under Graham Henry, it was the Achilles heel of this All Black team, and would undoubtedly be a target for top sides at the World Cup. Oliver's post-match comments were also concerning. He put down the four lineouts stolen from the All Blacks throw-in to them being so keen to get quality ball at the back of the lineout. For the second half he said this approach was altered to concentrate more on securing possession, even if it meant just hitting jumpers near the front. These lessons seemed to be taking a long time to learn — much longer than you'd expect from the top-ranked side in world rugby.

It was also interesting that while Oliver was being picked to start matches largely due to his strong scrummaging, there were no scrums fed by the All Blacks in the whole of the first half.

A controversial aspect of the match came ten minutes into the second half when Stirling Mortlock was penalized for a high tackle on Doug Howlett, which enabled the All Blacks to grab an 18 – 12 lead. The Australians rightfully felt hard-done-by with this decision; however, the All Blacks might have scored a try three minutes later if it hadn't been for referee Nigel Owens making a mistake the other way by calling McCaw for a knock-on off his head.

Undoubtedly the first refereeing blunder swung the momentum of the game slightly away from the Australians. The superior All Black bench and the impact from Mealamu and Leonard meant they were always likely to take control of this match. Both players were heavily involved in the build-up to the first try from Tony Woodcock, who crashed over in the corner from a pick-and-go in the 54th minute.

A 73rd minute Carter penalty was the last score in the game and took the All Blacks out to their 26 – 12 victory. Carter's kicking, both for line and goal, was one of the real highlights for the All Blacks, especially considering some tricky conditions. It was a relief to see the star returning to form, as he would need to be at the top of his game if the All Blacks were to win the World Cup.

Graham Henry continued his concerning habit of throwing players on late in the match when Nick Evans was given four minutes at fullback at the end of the game. Once again it proved to be ridiculous, as Evans kicked out on the full in his first touch of the ball.

THE THIRTY-MAN WORLD CUP SQUAD

On Sunday 22 July, Henry named his World Cup squad.

Backs: Mils Muliaina, Leon MacDonald, Doug Howlett, Joe Rokocoko, Sitiveni Sivivatu, Isaia Toeava, Conrad Smith, Luke McAlister, Aaron Mauger, Daniel Carter, Nick Evans, Byron Kelleher, Brendon Leonard, Andrew Ellis.

Forwards: Rodney So'oialo, Chris Masoe, Richie McCaw (capt), Jerry Collins, Sione Lauaki, Reuben Thorne, Ali Williams, Chris Jack, Keith Robinson, Carl Hayman, Neemia Tialata, Tony Woodcock, Anton Oliver, Keven Mealamu, Andrew Hore, Greg Somerville (provisional on recovering from injury).

The announcement of the squad featured the bombshell that Piri Weepu had been dropped for Andrew Ellis. In the weeks preceding the announcement, not one print, radio or television journalist had predicted this would happen. In times where leaked teams are nearly as prevalent as leaky homes, this was a big shock. To Weepu's credit he took the news well, choosing wisely to get a match of Air New Zealand Cup rugby for Wellington behind him before making any comment. Even then he was guarded, in the knowledge that an injury could see him back in the squad.

The general feeling was that Piri Weepu got a raw deal. He had shown some poor form, but also he had been given very limited opportunities to improve his form — the selectors' conditioning and rotation policies arguably more at fault than anything over which he had any control. If there is one player who would look back and be more frustrated with the conditioning window than anyone else, it would be Weepu. It wasn't that he didn't get good results. He reportedly lost 7 kg in the period, which was exactly what he'd wanted to do. However, on his return to rugby, the Hurricanes played him at first-five more than they did at halfback. At the time Weepu said the move was covered off with the All Black bosses and one that they were very positive about. But it was a move that would ultimately mean he'd play only a handful of matches of Super 14 and international rugby at halfback in the lead-up to the World Cup.

On the Thursday night before the final Tri-Nations test he was one of six players who went out on the booze and didn't get back to the team hotel until four in the morning. Five of the six missed out on the squad, leading to the conjecture that this contributed to Weepu's dropping. Like most of the speculation that surrounds the All Blacks it was irrational, and difficult to believe when Conrad Smith, another of the six curfew-breakers, was named in the team. Equally as irrational in my opinion was Henry's statement that Ellis had played so well for the New Zealand Junior team that he had to be included. That team had played poor opposition, and it could be strongly argued that Cowan was the form halfback ahead of Ellis.

The action of dropping Weepu was an admission that the selectors had been playing the wrong type of halfback almost right through their tenure.

It seemed more logical that Weepu had been dropped because Brendon Leonard was playing so well and bringing a different type of game to the All Blacks. Leonard's pass was quicker, more assured and, most importantly, Dan Carter looked better outside him. Weepu and Kelleher are very similar halfbacks and very different from both Leonard and Ellis.

Kelleher was fortunate to hold his position. His greater experience and his membership in the team's leadership group possibly gave him the nod for selection ahead of Piri. Certainly Byron's dreadful performance in the first half of the Bledisloe Cup decider at Eden Park would have thrown further doubts in the selectors' minds.

The action of dropping Weepu was an admission that the selectors had been playing the wrong type of halfback almost right through their tenure. With all the planning, experimentation and rotation that had taken place over the previous four years, neither Ellis nor Leonard had started in a test. The selectors hadn't been afraid to drop Weepu at the last minute. Would they now have the courage to make Leonard their number-one halfback for the Cup?

One other surprise selection was Sione Lauaki. This was a big call from Henry, who only months earlier had suggested Lauaki did not play for eighty minutes and needed more consistency in his game. A knee injury later prevented him from showing any type of form that would warrant selection. The only conclusion that can be reached is that the selectors changed their minds and decided they wanted a big man to have as an impact player.

The player to make way for Lauaki's inclusion was Troy Flavell. Flavell was outstanding in the early stages of the Super 14, but not so effective later against the bigger South African packs. In the tests of 2007 he could not recapture his early season form and looked jaded. The selectors chose Thorne ahead of him, preferring the Canterbury man's reliability and dependability. It was a surprising choice given that Graham Henry was largely responsible for encouraging Troy to return to New Zealand from Japan. Henry had always been a fan of Troy, consistently wanting to highlight the player's athleticism and skills.

The other most unlucky player to miss out on the squad was Rico Gear. Gear is a more complete winger than Doug Howlett, but Howlett edged him out through superior form in the Super 14 and being recognized as a good team man.

Apart from sympathy for Weepu, the team was generally well-received. In some positions it was extremely strong although questions remained about the strength at halfback and centre. There was also the nagging doubt of why there was no back-up to Richie McCaw at openside flanker.

The All Black thirty-man squad for the World Cup was confirmed on Tuesday 14 August. Greg Somerville claimed the 30th and final spot after being given extra time to prove he was fully recovered after an Achilles tendon operation had sidelined him for most of the season.

'We can't wait, fifteen days and we're on the plane,' was Graham Henry's comment.

The World Cup

'You learn off other people and they've been bold enough and straight enough to tell me what my faults are. I've listened most of the time, which has been a difficult thing for me.' — Graham Henry

No one expected the All Blacks would be out of the World Cup without even making the semi-final, and certainly not my publishers. The space that would have carried the match reports for the semi-final and final games has instead been used for my post-Cup analysis. It does not match the Contents listing, which was already printed in anticipation of a happier outcome.

THE WEEK BEFORE the All Blacks left New Zealand for the World Cup I interviewed Graham Henry. He was surprisingly relaxed for a man about to embark on the tour on which the success of his coaching career would be judged. I questioned him about his change of coaching style. His admissions of the change and the reasons for it led to one of the most revealing interviews I've had with him.

The World Cup is what everything is hingeing on. John Graham says this is the defining moment for G.W Henry's coaching career. Do you view it that way?

No, I just think about trying to do the job better each day and focus on making sure we do things right. If we do things right today we'll play well tomorrow. We are always trying to improve what we are doing on and off the field. We put a lot of thought into what we are doing for the Rugby World Cup and it's occupied my mind. I find that very stimulating. We're also trying to improve what we do off the field because we are away for fifty-three days and we need to enjoy each other's company and have good balance. We need to have other interests outside rugby, otherwise we're going to go up the wall. All those things are important.

They may be important but at the end of the day the whole thing is going to depend on results, isn't it?

If you don't get those things right you're not going to get the results. They are the foundation of those results. We understand that results are everything and I've been very aware for thirty years that it is results that count. You don't play for the scoreboard. You play to produce a performance and the scoreboard will look after itself.

You have a mantra which is basically that 'Good coaches win'. Presumably bad coaches lose. Is that what it is all about?

I think you have to think about the end result, otherwise you don't have a job. That is the reality. I'm a very competitive person. I think I give that persona off to the people I coach — it's very important that we produce the goods to produce the result. I think that is a very important part of a coach's strategy to win games. You need to have that competitive edge as an individual to get the best out of the people around you.

Now 2004 was a critical time in your coaching career. You came off losses in the Tri-Nations and the Bledisloe and went ahead in a different way. Is that a watershed in your career?

I think it was a watershed in this team's development. You need to find out how the team functions, what the culture's about, how individuals handle the pressures of international rugby and how they handle all the pressures of being an All Black. Quite frankly I hadn't had that experience. Most of the people in the management group hadn't either. We learnt from that and we changed a number of things.

Did you change?

I think we became more consensus. We started the dual management of the All Blacks. A leadership group was formed and they, with the management of this side, have managed the All Blacks over the last three years. I think that was a critical step in the right direction, the development of self-reliance and individual leadership. The coaching group probably put too much pressure on the players during the week. We probably over-trained them and didn't get them involved enough coaching themselves. So we decreased the amount of contact time. The development of the leadership group within the All Blacks has been hugely significant. That dual leadership has been a backbone of the development of this team.

This is a hard thing for a bloke to do who has been highly competitive and a principal, who believed in teacher-centred education to suddenly stop and change?

I think the rest of the management found me fairly difficult at times. I think they're reasonably pleased with the end result. You learn off other people and they've been bold enough and straight enough to tell me what my faults are. I've listened most of the time, which has been a difficult thing for me. Also you have to change with the way the players change. This group of players is quite different to the Blues team I coached in 96/97, they've come through a different education system, a different society and their values are different. If you coached the way you did ten years ago, they wouldn't be able to handle it. You just have to change with the times and the personalities you are coaching.

WIN	LOSS	Date	9 September 2007
1	**0**	Venue	Marseilles
		Against	Italy
		Score	76 – 14

In any tournament it's important to get off to a good start and the All Blacks did exactly that with a compelling victory marked by power, enterprise, enthusiasm and skill. MacDonald started at fullback with Muliaina at centre rather than Toeava, and without Thorne there was a lack of specialised cover on the bench.

It was a harsh call not to play Rokocoko, who would have benefited from time on the park and it could have been Leonard's first test start — that it wasn't seemed to indicate Kelleher would always start, no matter how well Leonard played. After a 23 – 20 loss to Ireland, the Italians were expected to compete with the All Blacks in some areas, but any plans they might have had were blown away within minutes. The men in black were like caged lions let loose in a supermarket full of eye-fillet. They devoured the Italians, tempering their assault in a calculating and clinical manner. The Italians were in a different league, and the All Blacks entered half-time with a 43 – 7 lead.

The second half saw Hayman sin-binned for punching an Italian forward. Presumably the other leaders in the team ripped into him later, as a similar lack of discipline against better opposition could prove disastrous. Despite being a man down, Jack scored and when Howlett touched down twice in three minutes, at 62 – 7 the match was effectively over.

WIN	LOSS	Date	15 September 2007
2	**0**	Venue	Lyon
		Against	Portugal
		Score	108 – 13

While Portugal faced a thrashing by the All Blacks, their passionate singing of their national anthem showed what it meant to play the dominant team in world rugby, as their fans sang and danced throughout the match.

From an All Black perspective, the most value for Henry's men was match fitness, so it was disappointing to see Muliaina off with a hamstring strain, while Smith made it through without re-injuring his hamstring, a huge relief for the coaching staff.

WIN	LOSS	Date	23 September 2007
3	**0**	Venue	Edinburgh
		Against	Scotland
		Score	40 – 0

When are the All Blacks not the All Blacks? When they wear silver lycra and look like rejects from the Warriors' cheer squad. The only thing worse than the All Blacks' jerseys were the Scottish ones, and the fact that players, spectators, touch judges and the referee couldn't tell the difference added to the confusion.

The match was never going to be a genuine contest after Scotland rested its first-string players for their game against Italy, so when McCaw scored after only four minutes it seemed as though the weakened Scottish team would pay dearly. But again the All Blacks lacked continuity, with an error rate that would prove fatal against stronger opposition. When Howlett touched down to become the All Blacks' highest try-scorer, it coincided with MacDonald picking up a thigh injury, forcing Evans on at fullback, where his performance showed his lack of game time. One of the most concerning aspects was Carter's poor goal-kicking. He desperately needed game time to get his goal-kicking and general play back to their very best.

WIN	LOSS	Date	29 September 2007
4	**0**	Venue	Toulouse
		Against	Romania
		Score	85 – 8

The week leading up to the All Blacks' last pool match was dominated by concerns about their preparation for the tougher matches. The high error count against Scotland; a mid-week 'holiday' and extensive rotation despite concerns from ex-All Blacks that he needed to play his top team to prepare them for the quarter-final — all had fans questioning Henry's approach.

One of the most outspoken critics was former coach Laurie Mains. 'The lack of rotation of key players like Carl Hayman, Richie McCaw and Dan Carter makes the rotation policy pointless. They haven't got depth in the three most crucial positions. Henry is not only throwing confusion into the opposition but now they're confusing their support base as well.'

The coaching staff were faced with a difficult reshuffle after Carter withdrew with a calf strain, and with injuries to Muliaina and MacDonald, McAlister was promoted from the bench. While the All Blacks talked up the Romanians' physicality, passes were thrown that never would be considered against tougher teams. In reality the World Cup wouldn't start for Henry's men till the following week. You'd think he'd have it all planned, but when asked about preparation for the next seven days, he said, 'Haven't thought about it yet. We'll get there.' With blind faith in Henry, the fans kept their fingers crossed. Answers like this, however, did nothing to put the nation at ease as the big games drew near.

WIN	LOSS		
4	1	Date	7 October 2007
		Venue	Cardiff
		Against	France
		Score	20 – 18

With France as their quarter-final opponent the All Blacks, untested since the Tri-Nations, were about to take on the Six Nations Champions. Whether the All Blacks' preparation had been ideal remained questionable, but it was widely thought France playing away from home wouldn't pose a serious threat.

The naming of the All Black side was eagerly awaited, as Graham Henry had rarely selected his top team during the last year, with most interest focused on whether Dan Carter would play following his calf injury, and the ever contentious midfield selection.

With Carter declared fit, McAlister and Muliaina were selected to start outside him, significant in that Muliaina was brought into centre at such a late stage of the tournament. More than anything it showed the coaching staff simply didn't have confidence that the two specialist centres in their squad — Smith and Toeava — were capable of doing the job. This decision became even more significant when the French named their team, electing to go with big punters of the ball at fullback and first-five, clearly planning on kicking a lot of ball long before pressurising those who returned it. With no Muliaina to threaten from the back, this tactic would prove worthwhile.

The match couldn't have started worse for the French with Serge Benson concussed in a tackle after only five minutes and having to be replaced.

A great first half by McAlister saw him feature in one of the All Blacks' few highlights, when he created and finished the only try of the first half. This came just a minute after desperate French defence bundled Williams into touch before he crossed the line. For McAlister it would be a case of hero to zero, as a harsh yellow card for obstruction five minutes into the second half swung the momentum of the match away from the All Blacks, when the French capitalised on the opportunity and tied the match up at 13-all while he was in the bin.

Williams was the star player for the All Blacks, largely responsible for the All Blacks stealing five of the French throws to the lineout while managing to win every one of their own throws. This lineout dominance translated to a 71 per cent share of possession and 63 per cent of territory for the All Blacks. In the recent past, lineout problems losing valuable possession had been the most costly area of the All Blacks' game. This time they won possession, but let themselves down by kicking away nearly as much ball as the French kicked their way. This showed through in the statistics, where the All Blacks kicked 38 balls from first-five to France's 41, and it was soon clear that Carter wasn't anywhere near his peak fitness or form. He eventually hobbled from the field after fifty-six minutes, at the same time as Kelleher was replaced by Leonard.

In contrast to Carter, France's star fly-half in recent years, Frederic Michalak, set up the match-winning try for the French with eleven minutes to go. He'd come off the bench just one minute before and showed he still had the gas to make the crucial line-break and the composure to wait for his support on the inside. Yannick Jauzion scored and Jean-Baptiste Elissalde kicked the crucial conversion, giving France the lead for the first time.

The final quarter of the match was meant to be where Graham Henry's very different team preparation was meant to come in to its own. Instead it was shown to be fatally flawed.

As the All Blacks rolled on their substitutes, the team that already lacked cohesion began to look like fifteen individuals trying to take on the tenacious French defence on their own. If one-off running really was the way the All Blacks wanted to win, where were the Nonus, the Weepus and the Lauakis, who could have really threatened the French?

The All Blacks' desperation and fatal disorganisation was summed up in the final minute when Luke McAlister had a wild attempt at a drop-kick, without any concerted effort by the team to work their way into position for a match-winning field-goal. Too desperate, too little and much too late. The French had done it again.

The verdict

The following account of the All Blacks' final game at the 2007 Rugby World Cup was written in my hotel room immediately after I finished watching the game. It reflects the culmination of my analysis of Henry's four-year campaign, and, in my opinion, answers the burning question I saw in the eyes of my fellow Kiwis in the stand in Cardiff. How could it have happened again?

We choked. Just at the time when we needed to perform . . . we choked. When the eyes of the rugby world were upon us, at a time when a champion team would step up, opposed by a team that just weeks earlier had been humiliated by Argentina . . . we choked. There is no other word for it . . . choked, choked, choked.

Immediately after the game, Graham Henry said that this was not the time to resign and he was proud of his All Blacks. On both counts he was wrong. John Hart at least had the class to resign the morning after his team was defeated in 1999 and before they played the meaningless game against South Africa.

The best that can be said about Henry's claim that he was proud of his All Blacks is that this was misplaced loyalty. Sadly, in my view, it highlighted that the coach had become so close to his team that he had lost his sense of objectivity. How could a coach of thirty years' experience claim to be proud of a team who had been humiliated without firing a shot?

Henry was in good company. TV3 featured on its Sunday evening news a poll it conducted in the hours following the game. Over 55 per cent of those polled believed that the referee was more responsible for the defeat than anyone else. This was greeted with indignant disdain by both Paddy O'Brien, manager of referees for the IRB, and Laurie Mains, former All Black coach. Both reacted with pragmatism and objectivity by saying it was time New Zealanders grew up.

This was not a case of a great French team beating the All Blacks, more that the New Zealanders beat themselves. The game clearly exposed two of Henry's key policies, which failed when the real test and true pressure were applied.

Rotation was a disaster. Throughout the quarter-final the All Blacks attacked in ones and occasionally twos, unable to fall back when pressure was applied on combinations forged by playing together week after week, month after month. Nowhere was this more apparent than in the midfield where the best fullback in the world, Mils Muliaina, was playing his first game for months at centre. Putting rotation aside, this selection itself was ill-advised given that the French had signalled their intention to kick the ball to the All Black fullback when they selected Lionel Beauxis instead of Frederic Michalak at fly-half.

The All Black backline failed to display any fluidity, any instinctive feel, any understanding of what their mates inside and outside were going to do . . . in short, any combination. Rotation had resulted in the development of a number of individuals at the expense of developing a team. To watch highly talented young New Zealanders playing together not as a team but more as strangers will be the haunting memory of the 2007 World Cup.

In the forwards it was just as bad. Certainly the scrum and even the lineout were strong but at ruck and maul time the All Blacks rarely drove forward as a pack. Their second-half emphasis became one-off 'pick and go' from the ruck. It was ineffective, time-consuming and unimaginative. They had played so little together they were incapable of regrouping and trying something different. Meanwhile the Fijian speedsters on the wing were nullified, brought in as additional one-off runners. Rotation was persisted with right to the death knell with Henry almost emptying his bench, using individual talent over collective unity and understanding. Watching the fiasco, as thousands of Frenchmen screamed *Allez Bleus!*, the cliché 'a champion team will always beat a team of champions' rang true. You could add 'an average team will beat a team of champions', particularly when the team of champions has had limited time playing together.

Rotation failed, with the quarter-final emphasising that the policy had been too selective. One of the few successes of the 2007 All Blacks was Nick Evans yet he was given little game time. Some months out from the Cup, Wayne Smith acknowledged the selectors had erred in not picking Evans more often but little was done to give him more game time. Instead, Carter regularly started as first five-eighth although many critics pointed out in the lead-up to the World Cup that such selective rotation was hypocritical. When Carter was injured in the quarter-final, Nick Evans was forced to come on at a critical stage in the match and although his performance was adequate, he was just another All Black who would have been better with more game time.

A combination of the rotation policy and the conditioning policy meant the All Blacks were not battle-hardened going into the World Cup. Clearly the idea and particularly the timing of the conditioning was flawed. The players were treated in a soft way, pampered and wrapped in cotton wool. Two in particular were given special treatment. Conrad Smith played only three minutes of test rugby in 2007 leading up to the World Cup. His contribution at the Cup itself reflected that. Keith Robinson, revered as a tough man, could only last fifty minutes against France. Neither Robinson nor Smith should have been selected.

The end result of conditioning was that the All Blacks looked bigger and more bulky, but at what cost? Gone was their instinctive athleticism, their innate ability to find space, their silky skills, their unpredictability, their intuitive flair . . . in other words all the qualities that had made them the most exciting and explosive team in the world. In my view, they were now just another bunch of pumped up professional sportsmen, so compartmentalised that someone else told them how to think, someone else told them how to kick, run and wipe their bum.

The timing of the conditioning window in February only makes sense to its instigator. When it was first announced, little mention was made of the other conditioning window after the Super 14 ended. This second window proved to be a week longer, with no New Zealand franchise making the final. Despite some camps being held, concern was starting to be expressed by a few outspoken critics. Leading the way was Laurie Mains, who consistently argued that players needed to play regularly to be match fit and to develop combinations. For the first time, journos like Wynn Gray in the *New Zealand Herald* began to use the term 'wrapped in cotton wool' when referring to the conditioning programme.

One of the benefits claimed by proponents of conditioning was that it would help the All Blacks avoid injuries and recover from them more quickly. Injuries to Smith, Robinson, Rokocoko, Carter, MacDonald, Mauger, Thorne, Eaton, Williams, Somerville, Muliaina, Mealamu, Jack, Tialata and Collins made a mockery of the claim.

Both Henry and Enoka emphasised in interviews the importance of developing a leadership group in the squad. They spoke glowingly of the contribution this group was making to the direction the squad was taking. Sir Brian Lochore was involved as a mentor to this group. It now seems clear that Henry and Enoka were deluding themselves. On the evidence of the quarter-final this was a leaderless team, a bunch of individuals without direction and no one obvious to follow.

Richie McCaw is an outstanding flanker, rivalling the great Michael Jones in this position, but his captaincy qualities appear to be limited. At no stage in the quarter-final did he pull the troops together, impress on them the seriousness of the situation, change the tactics or marshal his forces. His own play was impressive but his captaincy non-existent. His team constantly took wrong options, kicking far too often in the first half and persisting with pointless one-off running in the second. He will always be an automatic choice as flanker but the new coach would be wise to go for a new captain.

A further flaw that had been somewhat disguised by rotation was exposed in the quarter-final. Poor selections. The selection of Leon MacDonald at fullback took away the instinctive running and brilliant counter-attacking that Mils Muliaina brings in the number 15 jersey. Worse still, Mils was asked to slot in at centre for the first time in months. If the selectors had in fact known what they were doing and been prepared to act decisively, they would have selected a specialist centre to replace Tana Umaga. In fact an ideal replacement was ignored. Anthony Tuitavake, the North Harbour centre, has been a form player for the last two seasons. Ma'a Nonu, despite his handling problems, would have been a better bet than either Conrad Smith or Isaia Toeava. The selectors got the centre position wrong, simply repeating the mistakes of 1999 when Christian Cullen was wasted there and 2003 when Leon MacDonald was played out of position at centre. For a rugby nation to make the elementary mistake of playing a player out of position once is acceptable, twice is inexcusable while thrice is inexplicable. When it is the same position, a fullback playing centre, I believe the competency of the selectors has to be questioned.

Equally surprising was the dropping of Doug Howlett for this key game. He appeared to have played so well he was the number one winger and then out of the blue he was dropped, not even required on the bench. However, the most contentious selection was that of McAlister ahead of Mauger at second five-eighth. Mauger brings experience and a level head to the position while McAlister is an intuitive player who often takes the wrong option. In the quarter-final Luke went from try-scoring hero in the first half to yellow-carded zero in the second. While he was serving his ten minutes in the sin bin, France scored and got right back into the game. There is a strong argument to suggest Mauger was needed to bring direction and solidarity to the backline. In a team almost devoid of leaders, Mauger may have been able to settle the backs down in those final ten minutes when all remnants of formation and structure were lost.

Throughout his tenure Graham Henry persisted with Byron Kelleher at halfback. Byron's rugged athleticism and his outstanding defence are, in my view, sadly negated by his inability to read the game and his extreme emotionalism that causes him to lose the plot at times concentrating on personal battles instead of team objectives. Kelleher was selected ahead of Weepu, Cowan and, yes, Justin Marshall. Justin is playing his rugby in England and was consequently ineligible . . . a luxury the NZRU will not be able to stick with in the future.

The selection issues in the forwards for the quarter-finals were Anton Oliver ahead Keven Mealamu, and Keith Robinson instead of Chris Jack. Keven's non-selection became a non-issue when he was declared unfit the day before the game. It isn't so much the selection of Robinson after so little rugby as the inability of the coaches to motivate Chris Jack that causes concern. Jack, quite simply, was off the boil throughout all of 2007. He was badly injured during the Super 14 and was really a passenger from then on. This was a player who had been New Zealand Player of the Year as a comparative youngster, a person referred to in the same sentence as the great Colin Meads. His drop off in form should have been addressed because Chris Jack was the potential cornerstone of this pack. The fact that he didn't make the grade is something he and forward coach Steve Hansen have to live with.

Was this team underdone? There is no question that the All Blacks of 2007 were not a shadow of 2006 or 2005. On no occasion in 2007 did the All Blacks play to the level they achieved against the Lions two years earlier. They went backwards. Players like Collins, Hayman and Woodcock, who thrive on tough work week in and week out, quickly fell out of form. This type of All Black needed tough physical matches before the quarter-final but quite simply didn't get them.

Rugby players are no different from any other profession. They need to be playing rugby to be on top of their game. For them to be confident in their own ability, in their fitness, in their combination with their mates and in their team, they must be playing regularly. This All Black team got out of the routine of playing rugby, of being battle-hardened and of being tough and fit. By wrapping the team in cotton wool, over a period of time, inevitably their standard fell away.

What disguised this were the results. They continued to win throughout 2007 with the exception of Melbourne but these were wins without authority, without conviction. This was a team that had clearly peaked and was on its way down the other side.

Why did Henry not stop this? In my view he had become too close to the team, too insular, too removed from criticism. Graham seemed to turn more and more to those dependent on him for advice and predictably they told him what they thought he wanted to hear. For the first time he became defensive when questioned by the media, particularly about rotation and conditioning. This led in turn to some influential members of the media no longer bothering to interview him. What was the point when the whole country jumped down your throat with accusations of negativity and undermining the All Black effort the moment you questioned the party line?

The key question will probably always remain unanswered. Did Henry's deliberate and conscious change of coaching style ultimately lead to his demise? Gilbert Enoka is adamant that Graham would have lost the entire group if he had not changed. Henry himself believes it was important to empower the leadership group and to spread responsibility.

Henry has been most successful when he has had hands on, when he has been in control, when he has been planning, manipulating, scheming . . . in short, when he has been coaching.

There is a suspicion he lost control and in so doing this squad received mixed messages. Only Graham will know whether he felt comfortable sharing his duties with others. This is a coach who at his peak was in sole charge, in complete control; a man issuing simple, uncomplicated commands that he expected to be obeyed. Can you really change the habits of a lifetime?

One positive result of the Henry era is the large number of quality players to emerge. In Carter, McCaw, Leonard, Woodcock, Williams and Collins, New Zealand has a nucleus of talented All Blacks close to their peak. The NZRU would do well to tie these players into contracts to combat the after-effects of this World Cup campaign.

What was the cost? 2007 was the worst year for New Zealand rugby since 1999. The Super 14 became a farce from the moment the All Blacks were withdrawn from its early stages. The failure of any New Zealand franchise to make the final was symptomatic of what was to follow. The Air New Zealand Cup lost a lot of its interest when the All Blacks were out.

The test series against France C should have been cancelled. Did France con us? Canada simply weren't up to scratch and once South Africa withdrew its top players from the Tri-Nations, that too became farcical. The end result was that although the All Blacks won the Bledisloe and Tri-Nations Cups, they arrived for the ultimate test without the necessary season of tough games. They were underdone and they played accordingly. Add to that the substandard matches against opposition like Italy, Scotland, Romania and Portugal and the All Blacks were ripe for the picking.

It is important to again reiterate that Graham Henry was given everything he asked for. A huge support team, unlimited funding, the green light to rotate players and condition them — all, sadly, were not the answer. In reality, some if not all of these factors contributed to the worst ever performance by an All Black team at the World Cup.

The NZRU must also look closely at itself. It approved the policies that became the downfall of the team. I believe the board is as culpable as Messrs Henry, Hansen, Smith and Sir Brian Lochore.

Thousands of New Zealanders saved to go to the World Cup.

In most cases the cost of airfares, tickets to the games and accommodation would have cost them between $25,000 and $30,000 alone. The number who publicly vowed never to spend any money on the All Blacks ever again would be well in excess of the biggest crowd to go to an Air New Zealand Cup game this year.

The NZRU and the All Blacks need to realise that they must change their attitude to their stakeholders. The privileged position rugby has enjoyed in New Zealand for so long is under threat. Fans felt cheated, ripped off, frustrated by a team that wimped out without firing a shot. If the team hurt half as much as the fans crying in the stadium after the game they would have been distraught.

This was worse than the 1999 fiasco. This was a team without any apparent weakness except at centre. In 2005 and 2006 this team had played some sensational rugby but now all that was forgotten. On the only stage that really mattered, this team choked.

And what of Graham William Henry? How will he be remembered? Obviously his record over the four years was very good but so was John Mitchell's. Mitchell got his team through to the semi-finals, Henry didn't. Graham will be shattered by that result. This, after all, was what he had worked for, what he had trained for, what he had schemed about, manipulated for and contrived. In the end, he failed . . . dismally.

At the end of the game at Cardiff the words of Graham Henry's mentor and friend, former All Black captain John Graham, came to mind: 'This is the definitive moment of Graham Henry's coaching career.'

Henry failed because he made some basic errors. Rotation, conditioning and selection all let him down. Did he fail because he became a different style of coach, one inviting everyone to contribute with the end result that no one knew quite what was happening or who was in charge? Only he can answer that.

Graham Henry is fond of saying 'Good coaches win.' He didn't win at the World Cup when it really mattered. The All Blacks choked.

FAITH IN THE COUNTRYSIDE

**A Report presented to
The Archbishops of Canterbury
and York**

ACORA PUBLISHING

Cover photograph:
Mike Williams, by courtesy of the Countryside Commission

266
FCS

Faith in the Countryside
was first published in 1990 by
Churchman Publishing Limited
117 Broomfield Avenue
Worthing, West Sussex BN14 7SF

Copyright by
The Archbishops' Commission on Rural Areas,
1990 (ACORA)

Represented in
Dublin; Sydney; Wellington;
Kingston; Ontario and Wilton, Connecticut

Distributed to the book trade by
ACORA Publishing
The Arthur Rank Centre
National Agricultural Centre
Stoneleigh Park
Warwickshire CV8 2LZ

ISBN 0 9516871 1 5

Typeset and printed by
Bourne Press Limited, Bournemouth